HER NAME
IS
MONTEL

CASEY M. EVANS

Outskirts Press, Inc.
Denver, Colorado

Her Name is Montel
All Rights Reserved

Outskirts Press
http://www.outskirtspress.com

ISBN-10: 1-59800-229-5
ISBN-13: 978-1-59800-229-4

Library of Congress Control Number: 2005937271

Printed in the United States of America

DEDICATION

This book is dedicated to my son, Sean. Without the balance that he brings to our family, this work would not have been possible.

Casey M. Evans

TABLE OF CONTENTS

PREFACE

This book is neither wholly fiction nor wholly non-fiction – instead it is both. The first and last chapters, *Montel Mercedes Ranch* and *The Beginning*, are fictional and describe a ranch, a unique kind of care home that does not yet exist. But we hope someday that it will exist. The remaining chapters, or the body of the book, are my own true story of how I was changed by my daughter with special needs. These chapters are factually accurate and completely true as well as I can recall. All names throughout the story have been changed to protect people's privacy, with the exception of my immediate family: Casey, Delia, Sean and of course Montel.

The primary reason I have written this book is that while most people acknowledge the value of special needs people, they are still very segregated from most of us in our everyday lives. I believe the separation is a sad outcome for both us and them. If this book can touch the heart of even one reader and cause him or her to challenge our society's current paradigm of keeping developmentally disabled, elderly, or others arbitrarily isolated, then it will have been a success.

Thank you for reading my book,

CHAPTER 1
MONTEL MERCEDES RANCH

Julie McNeal turned her car off of the rural highway and onto a narrow county road. She was tired of driving and glad that according to her brochure they were now only two and a half miles from their destination. This would be the tenth care home that she and her daughter Audrey had looked into in the last two months. Julie began to wonder if her standards were unrealistically high and if she would ever find a place for her daughter.

Audrey was now thirty-one years old and had not spoken a word since she was three. The doctors had never been able to determine exactly what was wrong with Audrey. Julie's husband stayed with them for about one year after Audrey stopped talking, trying the whole time to convince Julie that something had to be done with Audrey or he would not stay. He kept insisting that Audrey would be better off somewhere else; that it was for her own good. Then one day he gave up trying to make Julie see it his way, and he left. Julie went to work as a dispatcher for a trucking company where her uncle worked and raised Audrey by herself from then on with plans of keeping Audrey at home forever. But now Julie recognized that she was getting older and Audrey was getting too big and too difficult for her to manage.

And so the family of two continued up the narrow country road. The road meandered through hills that were covered with tall, dry yellow grass that swayed in the wind, clumps of twisted red-barked manzanita bushes and large mature oak trees. The valleys were green from irrigation sprinklers and speckled with grazing cattle and horses. Julie was trying to keep optimistic and convince herself that this one might be different, but, as the road narrowed and became bumpier, she could not help but have her doubts. She started imagining a run-down farmhouse or even a mobile home in this area. Eventually the pavement ended altogether, and her hope for an ideal care home for Audrey became more remote. But Julie had heard good things about this place, and since they had come this far she decided she needed to check it out. And so she begrudgingly continued on the dirt road for about three hundred more yards, took a left and came upon the entrance to the ranch.

There was no mistaking the entrance. The road changed dramatically to a nicely paved two-lane road that wound its way up a small hill. And just to the right of the road where the pavement began was a large redwood sign with elegant curved letters carved into the wood. The letters were painted a gleaming white: "Welcome to Montel Mercedes Ranch."

Julie drove the car up the hill to what looked like a mountain resort hotel. It was an expansive redwood building with oversized windows. The grounds around the building were beautifully manicured with grass, small evergreen shrubs, and colorful flowers. An old-fashioned wagon in the middle of an entryway circle was filled with flowers and draped with colorful hanging plants.

A small man wearing a dark blue polo shirt and khaki shorts approached the car and opened the door for Julie.

"Welcome," he said. "May I park your car for you?"

"Thank you," Julie responded. The man's facial features and mannerisms made her think he probably had Down syndrome. Then she noticed a young Hispanic woman wearing the same type of dark blue polo shirt and khaki shorts who was watching everything from a booth near the entrance to the building. As Julie and Audrey walked toward the entrance, she smiled and said, "Welcome." She pointed towards a sign and then held out her hands as if waiting to receive something. The sign read: *While on these premises we ask you to challenge the status quo. Please check your preconceived ideas and biases here. We will gladly return them to you upon your departure.*

Not exactly sure of what to do, Julie grabbed at the air and handed the woman a fictitious object. The woman's smile let Julie know that the symbolic gesture was exactly what she had hoped Julie would do. She pretended to put the object under the small counter where she stood. "Gracias, and have a wonderful visit," she said as Julie and Audrey entered the building.

They stepped inside and were immediately surprised by the grandeur of the room. A large common area with polished hardwood floors was flanked on both sides by building wings that probably had nine rooms on each of their two stories. A sunken living room had cozy, large stuffed furniture and plenty of large pillows. Next to the fireplace was a polished black grand piano. The room's large windows provided a spectacular view of cascading blue and green rolling peaks of the Sierras. Julie thought it was more like being in an exclusive ski lodge than in a care home.

A pleasant looking blonde haired woman with a slight case of acne approached them. She wore the same type of dark blue polo shirt and khaki shorts as the parking lot attendants.

"Hi," she said, "My name is Brandy. You must be Julie?"

"Yes," Julie replied. "Nice to meet you Brandy, we are here to see a Mr. Evans."

Just then a large, slightly overweight man of about sixty years old bounded down the stairway. His rosy face was in stark contrast to the white hair of his head, mustache and full beard, as well as to his blue eyes. As he reached the bottom of the stairs, he revealed a mischievous looking crooked smile as he held out his hand to Julie.

"Hi there," he said. "I'm Casey Evans, founder and director of Montel Mercedes Ranch." His eyes twinkled, and he seemed to have an easy confidence that said to Julie this was truly a happy man.

"Did you have any trouble finding us?" he asked, with a knowing smile. Julie smiled back. One thing she was certain of: Anyone who made it out here for the first time would definitely find the journey memorable.

They chatted for some time and Julie noticed that he made eye contact and included Audrey equally in the conversation. Most people ignored Audrey when the two of them were together; but she noticed how respectful and comfortable he was with Audrey.

Finally he said, "I'm terribly sorry, but in a few minutes I am expecting a call. Would it be okay if Brandy shows you around?" Julie agreed, and so, after assuring them that he would talk to them later, he left and headed back up the stairs.

"Let me show you around a little bit," Brandy said. She explained that because it was a sunny and warm summer day no one wanted to be inside using the room right now, but in the winter the fireplace is stoked up and they all sit around singing and talking in the big room.

They left the common room through the set of French doors and stood on a patio that was at the top of a courtyard. The courtyard was a long gentle hill that swept down the center of the property. At the top of the hill was a grassy area with people sitting around picnic tables and barbequing. Beyond that, a circle of about ten people were sitting down on the grass while a young man and woman wearing the signature dark blue colored shirts led the group in singing songs while the man strummed a guitar. Beyond that group some adults and children played together in an area with sand, oversize swings, and a ping pong table. Finally, at the bottom of the courtyard was another building with the same redwood stained ranch-style look as the rest of the property.

Julie noticed a wide variety of people, not what she expected from a care home. There were young families, children, and grandparents. In fact, it was no different than a resort except for the fact that about every third or fourth person appeared to have some type of a disability and was accompanied by a blue-shirted staff person to assist him or her.

As they made their way down the hill, Audrey made a sign that she wanted to join the group that was singing in the middle of the courtyard. Even though she was non-verbal, she tugged at her Mom's shirt and gestured, communicating that she would like to sit with the group. Brandy indicated that it would not be a problem, but Julie had learned long ago to be very protective of Audrey. She cautiously surveyed the group, thinking that leaving Audrey alone in a new environment was probably not a good idea. She looked upon the group and could tell by facial expressions and mannerisms that about six of the people were disabled. What surprised her was that there was also a quite normal looking, white-haired older couple and two well-built young men among the group as well.

A tall young woman with ivory white skin wearing a colorful cotton summer dress stood up and approached them. She had a very unique look (her ears were set low on her head, and her face was very triangular) and was actually quite pretty in an unusual way. Julie thought she recognized the facial features as being associated with some type of genetic syndrome, but could not remember the name of it, or even if it was in fact a genetic syndrome that was associated with this woman's appearance.

The woman said to Julie, "Hi, I'm Rachel." Her speech was very nasally and difficult to understand. But she seemed sweet, and it was such a nice gesture to come over and greet them that Julie replied, "Nice to meet you Rachel, I'm Julie."

Apparently Rachel had sensed Julie's trepidation about leaving Audrey with the group because she leaned in close to Julie so as not to be overheard and said, "Don't worry, we're all used to being around people like your daughter." She looked at Julie with deep blue eyes that were filled with utter sincerity.

Julie laughed inside at the irony of Rachel's comment. This sweet young woman did not even consider that Julie might be concerned about the group, but instead assumed Julie must be worried about how they would all feel about Audrey. This new perspective made her feel silly for being so apprehensive in the first place.

"Thank you Rachel," Julie said. "I'm glad you are so open-minded." And she led Audrey over to the group, letting her sit down and join them. A simple nod of acknowledgement from the young man playing guitar indicated he was aware that she had joined them, and they would all watch out for her. The group seemed happy and content. Julie's instincts now told her that it was a safe environment, and she felt comfortable leaving Audrey with them.

Brandy and Julie continued to walk down to the building at the bottom of the courtyard. Brandy explained that it was called the *Activity House*. As they entered, it was obvious how it got its name. There were a set of picnic tables in the middle of the room. The walls were covered with an array of arts and crafts: brightly colored hand painted pictures, ice-cream sticks, leather purses and belts, Styrofoam balls covered with glitter and sequins and more. Waist-high cabinets that contained the paints, paper, glue, leather, scissors, glitter, and other supplies bordered the walls.

In one corner, a stunning piece of art made out of bits and pieces of broken glass reflected an artistic genius that Julie had rarely seen in her entire life. The broken chards of glass dangled and moved ever so slightly, causing light to burst and flash from its ever changing essence. Julie stared at it for several minutes.

Suddenly a middle-aged man with rumpled salt and pepper hair and two days of facial growth entered the room. He was followed closely by another slightly younger man and woman who were wearing bicycle pants, shirts, hats, and shoes. The athletic looking younger couple was in sharp contrast to the frumpy looking first man.

The first man approached Julie and Brandy and stood near them but at an angle turned slightly away from them, as if too shy to look directly at them. "I'mBob," the man said quickly.

"Bob is the artist of this piece," Brandy explained.

"I'mBob," the artist repeated excitedly.

"Wow! What an incredible work of art you have created,"

Julie said to him. "This is absolutely amazing!"

Still not able to look directly at her, but in an acknowledgement of her kind words, he smiled and said, "I'mBob," and patted his chest with his hand. Julie smiled and looked over at the other two people.

"Hi," the other man interjected after a brief silence. "My name is David and this is my wife Val. I'm Bob's brother."

"Whatareyadoin," Bob asked.

David smiled at Bob and then at Julie. He seemed very patient and kind to his brother.

"Nice to meet you everyone, I'm Julie."

"I noticed you come in earlier," David said to Julie. "Is that beautiful woman that you came in with your daughter?"

Julie was a little taken aback . . . she could not remember the last time someone described her daughter as beautiful.

"Yes," Julie said. "I am considering moving her here."

"That's great," David said. "This is a really good place. You will notice a change in her right away. When Bob first came here he was completely non-verbal, and would just sit in his room and rock back and forth for hours."

"Whatareyadoin," the brother interjected.

"Now look at him, he keeps real busy with his artwork, and we can't keep him quiet!" David said as he jokingly taunted his brother.

"Whatareyadoin," Bob said again, taking the bait.

"I'll tell you what I'm doin', buddy," David said playfully. "I'm going to get you!"

Bob laughed and started running out of the room.

"See you later Julie . . . it was nice meeting you," David called back to Julie as he left the room chasing after his brother.

Julie and Brandy watched them until they were wrestling around on the grassy courtyard outside of the room. Julie was struck by how accepting David was of his brother's disability.

The tour continued as they went through a side door that connected to the adjacent room, where every inch of floor was covered with thickly padded mats. There were large therapy balls, trapeze-like therapy equipment for stretching, and many large bean bag chairs. Outside this room offering another view of the rolling peaks of the Sierra mountain range were locker rooms and a large swimming pool. A large ramp on the shallow end of the Olympic-sized pool allowed wheelchairs to roll right into the pool. It was a warm summer day, and so the pool was bustling with people swimming and lounging about. There were children yelling, splashing each other and laughing.

Brandy then pointed out a paved, wheelchair friendly path, heading further down the hill. She explained that trails such as this one weaved throughout the property and led, for example, to the stables at the bottom corner of the property. Brandy told Julie that they had eight horses on the ranch and a petting zoo.

"There are also some ponds down there that fill up in the winter and spring time . . . but they are pretty much dried out by now," she said. "Let's head back up, and I'll show you the guest rooms."

"Guest rooms?" Julie asked.

"Yes," Brandy said. "We encourage relatives of the residents to visit as often as possible. We even provide them with some activities. For example, if you had someone come to visit Audrey who likes to golf, we provide him or her with a voucher for up to four people to go and play Golden Oak, the golf course nearby in Apple Hill. And we give visitors discounts on jet-ski rentals down at Folsom Lake. We even give them a dinner for two at one of the local restaurants. There are all kinds of things people visiting can do here and in the surrounding area."

Julie started to understand why there were so many people at the facility who did not appear to have any type of disability. They were all staying here as guests, making a vacation out of visiting their loved ones.

They walked back up the hill, entered the building, and went upstairs where Brandy unlocked a door. They entered a fully furnished two bedroom apartment and were greeted by golden rays of sunshine sweeping through the French doors at the back of the living room. The French doors led to a balcony that overlooked the courtyard and the Sierras. The living room's large overstuffed sofa, chairs, and tables sat on a large Persian rug surrounded by hardwood floor. A ceiling fan hung down from the tall open ceiling and turned lazily, circulating the air. Brandy opened an entertainment center along the wall, displaying a television and stereo.

The master bedroom had a four poster bed, dresser, and entertainment center. Several small house plants and indoor trees complimented the room's décor. A large bay window provided another exceptional view of the common area and rolling tree-topped peaks of the Sierras.

The apartment gave Julie the urge to kick her shoes off, sit in one of the cozy looking chairs and read a good book.

Brandy explained that if Audrey got into the home, Julie or anyone she authorized as a visitor of Audrey would be entitled to rent one of the apartments for a nominal fee. Julie started imagining all of Audrey's cousins, nieces, aunts, uncles and nephews who would love to come and stay in a place like this.

They left the apartment and proceeded to the director's office. He told Julie to come in and asked politely if she would like anything to drink as Brandy closed the door on her way out.

"So what do you think of the place?" he asked, as he gestured to one of the chairs in front of his desk.

"It's amazing!" Julie said as they both sat down.

"Do you think this may be the type of home you had in mind for Audrey?" he asked.

"Definitely," she said without hesitation.

"Good! I'll need to get you an application then," he said, as he started looking through his desk drawers.

"You must be proud," Julie said, gesturing towards the host of awards and community accolades on the wall.

"It definitely feels good to get recognition," the director said. "But you know what made me the most proud and made me feel like we truly had succeeded?" he asked, as he pulled out a large envelope and placed it on the desk.

Julie shook her head.

"My son now lives in Boulder, Colorado, with his wife and two children. He called to say they were coming to visit for Christmas several years ago. So I told him that I would prepare his old room at our house. The line got really quiet, and I could tell that he wanted to say something that was difficult for him to say. 'Well Dad,' he finally said, 'if it's all the same to you we would rather stay at the Ranch.' That to me was the greatest compliment and measure of our success. Because I knew that we had created a place where people like your daughter would not be forgotten and isolated. A place that was fun, where family and friends *wanted* to come and visit."

"You certainly have," Julie said. "I can't imagine anyone who wouldn't want to stay in a place like this. What ever made you decide to start up a home like this in the first place?"

"Well," he said, "that's a long story."

"Were you always sensitive to people with disabilities and wanting to help them?"

"Not at all," he said emphatically. "That's an even longer story."

Julie could not help but wonder what would inspire a man to create such an innovative place instead of leaving, the way her ex-husband had. She patiently looked at the director and said, "It is one o'clock in the afternoon and I don't have to leave until around six."

He smiled and chuckling said, "All right, but a story this long is going to require a pot of coffee."

He leaned over to a coffee maker sitting on a credenza, and pushed a button, illuminating a small red light. With the sound of the coffee machine gurgling in the background, the director sat at his desk, removed his glasses and rubbed his eyes. Then he looked thoughtfully into space and said, "We have to go back, way back, about thirty years ago . . ."

CHAPTER 2
EXPECTING

I was thirty-two years old and I loved my job. I was working as an Internal Auditor for a nationwide property management company auditing commercial real estate. I loved how important I felt as I walked onto a property and the employees immediately became filled with a mixture of fear and respect. I loved how it simplified everything down to black and white. Either procedures were being followed or they were not. My job was simple - I impartially and methodically recorded what I found. Since I am a very organized and methodical person by nature, I was very good at doing this.

But I especially loved my job because of the travel. I traveled throughout the United States for weeks at a time. I think I might have been compensating from some type of isolation issue resulting from growing up in a small town in Wyoming. I spent many days growing up being stuck inside because of the brutally cold weather and wishing I could be anywhere in the world besides where I was. All I know is that I continued to feel a sense of excitement and accomplishment each time I arrived home from, or packed up to leave on, a business trip.

It was late October and I was returning home to Oakland, California, on an afternoon flight from Dallas after a two-week trip. After an uneventful landing, I waited for the passengers in the rows in front of me to leave the plane before getting up to gather my carry-on bags and head for the baggage claim. I was restless and anxious to get off the plane. I turned the small circular air vent above my head open as far as it could go so that it was blowing the maximum amount of air, but the air still felt stuffy and stagnant. Yet I had to stay seated because there was no way my six-foot-tall frame could fully stand up underneath the overhead bins. Following what seemed like an unbearable amount of time, the row directly ahead gathered up their bags and scurried down the aisle. Finally it was my turn. I gathered my briefcase and laptop and headed down the aisle.

As I walked down the terminal, I laughed to myself at the people that were stopped squinting at the monitor to see where they needed to go to get their baggage. Being the experienced traveler that I was, I walked directly to the baggage claim area and looked for some familiar faces of my flight. Finding the carousel surrounded by passengers from my flight, I waited a few paces back - another mark of experience - as long as one can see the baggage clearly, the proximity to the conveyor belt does not speed up the process. I really enjoy watching people in these circumstances. I feel like a spy on a secret mission. Most of the people are so easy to read: the family visiting relatives, the college friends on a break, a retired couple on a small getaway. Excitement was in the air. I too was excited to be home, but I kept my exterior cool and aloof . . . just another routine business trip. In a few minutes I saw my large garment bag and I stepped up to the carousel and snatched it up.

I carried the laptop, briefcase, and garment bag outside and spotted my wife waiting by the curb. I had only been married a few months, so the idea of her being my wife still seemed new to me. Delia had been my girlfriend for years. We shared an apartment for longer than I can remember. Delia, my new wife, is a beautiful Filipina woman with golden brown skin, jet black hair, and striking dark eyes that dance with life. We kissed, loaded the bags and were ready to go. I automatically headed for the driver's seat, and she just as naturally moved to the passenger side. We left the airport and headed south for the twenty mile drive to our apartment.

Our apartment sat high in the hills of the East Bay overlooking the city of Hayward and the San Francisco Bay. We always had a delightful view, but as I weaved through the afternoon traffic, I anticipated the especially good view we would have in a few hours as we sat on our balcony and watched the sunset over the gleaming lights of the city and the Bay.

After some casual conversation, Delia turned to me and said with a forced, nonchalant tone, "Guess what?"

For some reason my mind flashed back to a dream I had the weekend before while in Dallas. In the dream, I was with a small boy who was my son. The weird thing about the dream was that I didn't seem to mind his company. I have always had a non-conformist streak, and that included at the top of the list *never* having kids. So as I woke up that morning it seemed odd to me that I had feelings of disappointment realizing that it was just a dream. I spent some time later that day driving aimlessly around sleepy Dallas neighborhoods taking special note of the children playing and allowing myself to wonder what it would be like to have children. I met with friends later that night, and I had not thought of the dream, or of parenthood again . . . until now.

"You're pregnant," I guessed.

"Oh my God!" she said. "How did you know?"

"It's a long story," I said. "Are you sure?"

"Yes," she said. "I took a home pregnancy test twice, and then I even went to the doctor."

I think I was in shock. I began to feel lightheaded. On one hand, I knew my life was going to change forever; but on the other hand, I felt as if it wasn't really happening at all, that it was a big joke.

"How do you feel about it?" Delia asked.

"Great!" I lied. But since I was not really sure how I felt yet, I figured I might as well not upset her. Besides, I did remember that it felt pretty good in the dream.

As we continued to drive home I realized it was hard for me to think of Delia as a mother. Delia has a very forceful and assertive personality. My stereotypical mother figure on the other hand is based upon my own mother . . . someone very soft-spoken and timid to the point that people sometimes take advantage of her. Delia is the exact opposite - she is strongly principled, and God help whoever does what she deems unfair. For instance, look what happened one time when we ordered a new bed and arranged to have it delivered two weeks later on a Sunday afternoon. When the delivery date came, we dutifully waited at home in the afternoon for the delivery. At around two o'clock, the doorbell rang, and a group of working men stood outside our door announcing that they were delivering our new bed. They removed our old bed and set up the bed frame and box springs mattress of the new bed. Then they announced very matter-of-factly, as if nothing in the world could be done about it, that the top mattress was not in stock, and they would be delivering it later in the week. I felt the situation was annoying, but that we might as well accept it and plan to sleep on the sofa or something for the next few days. Delia on the other hand was livid.

"This is not honoring our deal!" she told one of the delivery men. "You wait right here while I call the store," she told the man. The delivery man looked at me with a patient, exasperated expression and said under his breath so as not to upset Delia any more than she already was, "She can call anyone she wants to, but there is no way you will get that mattress any sooner." He was, however, clearly amused by the ensuing showdown between this irate customer and his management. He also realized that the battle gave him a mandatory break. So he sat down on our front step and lit up a cigarette. I decided to leave on a nearby errand, and as I left, I heard Delia on the phone demanding to talk to someone's supervisor.

When I returned a little later, I saw a man who looked vaguely familiar walking into our apartment carrying two pillows. Before I could even park, he was walking out again empty-handed and that is when I recognized him: It was the manager of the store where we bought the bed! I walked in and Delia had a look of triumph and satisfaction as she explained that they were delivering the other mattress later that afternoon and that the manager of the store just gave us two pillows and a set of sheets to make up for any inconvenience that the delay, which now was only going to be a few hours, may have caused. I looked over at the delivery guy who also looked smug and satisfied. He reiterated what the company agreed to, and did not hide his sense of joy in the fact that Delia had stood up to the management of his company, and won. It was now a victory for him and his co-workers as much as it was for us. I asked him, "Now do you see why I let her do all of my negotiating for me?"

He responded, "Now I see why you married her!"

We laughed, gave him and his crew a tip, and told them we would see them later when they delivered the top mattress. Later that day they did.

Delia is not intimidated by anyone. When we met, she bragged to me about how she would tell off the assistant managers at the automobile manufacturing plant where she worked as an administrative support staff if they did not fill out a form correctly. Now I was trying to imagine that I am about to become a father and she is about to become a mother. It was hard for me to imagine.

The next morning we woke up and drove to the mall. We actually waited for the mall to open just to go to the bookstore and get a baby-name book. By then I had explained to Delia about the dream of the small boy who was my son during my Dallas trip. We both had a feeling it was an omen and thought we would probably have a boy. So we concentrated mostly on boys' names.

Over the next several months everything seemed to revolve around the new baby. Actually, in my case, it revolved more around the excitement and anticipation of the new baby. The reality of actually having a child still had not sunk in. I was like a young girl filled with the excitement and joy of a wedding, planning every detail about the colors, flowers and music . . . all the while never considering the ramifications of being married.

For Christmas, in addition to gifts for Delia, I bought a teddy bear for the baby. For our anniversary, also in late December, besides an anniversary gift I bought baby clothes. But Delia was barely showing, and the prospect of being a parent still seemed very abstract and distant to me.

In the middle of February, my coworkers invited Delia to come to my work for a baby shower. I met her in the lobby of the large towering glass office building in Foster City where I worked when I was not on the road. We rode the elevator up thirty-five flights to my floor. We got off the elevator and made our way through a long hallway of shoulder-high cubicle partitions to the corner conference room that had large glass windows providing a view of San Francisco Bay and the San Mateo Bridge. On the large conference table in the middle of the room was a modest assortment of gifts, a cake, and a variety of soft drinks. The cake was a single layer cake the size of a cookie tray covered with white frosting and had *Congratulations* written in the middle of it with bright red frosted letters.

We were greeted by a dozen or more of my co-workers. Brad, the Assistant Controller, was a thin middle-aged man with a long grey pony-tail. Before this job he had spent years in the Navy. I believe spending so much time traveling and being around young men is why he remained young at heart. Janet was a frumpy woman with thick glasses who prided herself on reconciling every bank account, at every property, that the company owned or managed: we are talking a full time job of doing nothing but bank reconciliations. I think Janet was a librarian who missed her calling. Peggy was the zany Accounts Payable Supervisor. Peggy was a tall woman in her thirties who had decided to *not* age gracefully. Her flamboyant personality made her frequent hair color changes and brightly-colored, tight fitting clothes seem completely natural. John was a balding man in his early forties who was one of the company's General Ledger accountants. John worked at a local phone company for years and then got laid off and started to work with us a short time ago.

After chatting for some time, the conversation turned to if we were going to have a boy or a girl. And did we even know? I was embarrassed to mention the Dallas dream because I thought it would sound too mystical for a bunch of bean counters. But I saw no harm in telling them about the needle trick that I had learned from my sister. I had convinced myself that somehow due to our body's polarization or magnetic fields or for some other reason, the needle trick was very scientific, that it really was capable of predicting the sex of a baby. After all, every time I had tried the needle trick on Delia's belly it indicated that she was having a boy. And every time I tried it on other people it always seemed to work as well.

"The needle trick goes like this," I said. "You take about two feet of thread and tie a needle to one end. Then you hold on to the thread and allow the needle to dangle in the air. Now, once you get the needle to move in an oval pattern you hold very still, allowing it to continue its natural trajectory. Then, have someone else extend an open, flat hand as close to the needle as he or she can without touching it. The needle's pattern of motion will change from an oval to a circle for women . . . and from oval to straight back and forth for men."

We found a needle and some thread and started the experiment. First we had Delia lean back in a chair so that she was nearly lying flat. I dangled the needle and got it going in an oval pattern, slowly lowering it to just above her protruding belly. As if being held by a magnet, the needle jerked into a distinct straight back and forth motion. Everyone was fascinated but still skeptical.

So we tried it on several other people. Sure enough, every time a woman held her hand up to the dangling needle it would break out of its oval pattern into a circle. When several men tried, it would change into a straight back and forth motion. At that point I think we were all certain that we were going to have a boy.

Finally Lawrence Roberts, my boss and good friend,

wanted to give it a try. Lawrence was a small meticulous man who had the neatest office in the company. He dressed superbly with the best suits that complimented his always tan complexion, curly blond hair and blue eyes.

I got the needle going in an oval pattern and held my hand that tethered it as still as possible. Lawrence slowly raised an open hand so that the needle swung just above it. The needle went in a distinct circle, then it switched to straight back and forth, and then to a circle again! There was an awkward silence as the needle kept switching back and forth between the two patterns.

Finally Lawrence said with just enough slow Southern drawl to remind us that he was from Mississippi, "I guess I confused it." We all burst into laughter. You see, Lawrence was openly gay.

It was a magical time in my life when everything seemed festive and alive. Every day brought me further away from my old life and into the anticipation of parenthood and the new life. Countless moments were spent in the wonderment of what our baby would be like and how he would impact the world.

Slowly, the rainy cold nights of winter gave way to high overcast clouds and the chilly nights of spring. And by March we were making some major life changes in anticipation of our new addition due to arrive the first week of July. We moved from our luxury apartment high in the hills with a beautiful view of the Bay . . . to a conservative two-bedroom condominium in the valley, the same valley that we used to look at perched on our balcony high above. Delia's stomach protruded out to double or triple its usual size. She was looking like a woman who would have a baby any day . . . and we still had four months to go!

I still loved my job and hated the thought of doing anything more routine; but I felt if I made the sacrifice now I would probably be glad to be at home with the baby when it arrived. So I started looking for a position that would not require travel. I was sitting at my desk in early March when I accepted an offer with an Oakland-based property management company. It was located in a building that was the antithesis of the modern high-rise office building where I currently worked. It was a small two-story building in a neighborhood that warranted high profile black wrought iron security bars on every window of the building and parking garage. The interior was older too, with faded carpet and small cubicles that looked through the barred windows to the apartment building next door. That afternoon I gave my resignation to Lawrence. My job with all of its glamorous traveling was coming to an end. Even though I knew I would miss the job, the traveling, the glitzy building, and the expense account, the feelings of loss for the job were more than compensated for by the eagerness of starting a family. It felt as if forces of nature were taking over and parenthood was the next natural progression for my life.

One weekend in early April, Delia and I went to a baby store to complete the outfitting of our second bedroom. The room already had a crib, changing table, dresser drawers, rocking chair, and baby swing. The only thing left was bedding for the crib. Because of the dream I had in Dallas about having a little boy, the needle trick, and now even some sonograms that looked like there was a little something *down there,* I was completely convinced that we were having a boy. But since we had not found out for certain, and since we might have another baby someday, it seemed wise to get a theme that was neutral. We got a set called *Kelly's Kite.* Its colors were light green, yellow, and white, making it gender neutral. I also liked it because of its Irish theme, being of Irish heritage myself. The mobile had small knitted kites of every color and shape. The crib, dresser and changing table were all made from a matching light pine-colored wood. Now the baby's room was complete and there was nothing left to do but wait and daydream about the big day.

Driving to and from work, I would think to myself how it would be the day the baby was born. I absentmindedly rehearsed conversations I would soon be having with my family and friends. *Guess what? We just had a healthy seven pound, four ounce baby boy! Well, he has my nose and Delia's eyes . . .*

Then, in the middle of April, Delia went into a false labor. After spending two nights in the hospital, she was released but put on bed rest until the baby was born. I waited on her hand and foot as soon as I got home in the evenings until I left the next morning. I really did not mind all that much, but frankly it made me look forward even more to the day she would finally have this baby. She told me that she felt as if she had been pregnant forever. I tried to be a comfort to her . . . but it did seem like a lifetime ago when she met me at the airport and announced the news. I felt sorry for her because she generally likes to be very active and surrounded by people. Now she was immobile and isolated from everyone but me and a few close friends. She would hear about things at her work place and want to get involved, but knew that she was unable to. Rather, she had to continue to lie still and try to rest. I could see the frustration her immobility caused increase daily.

Finally when I came home on May 29th, Delia told me that she went to see the obstetrician and was told that the baby's lungs were mature enough, so they were going to admit her into the hospital two days later and induce labor. It sounded to me like a customary decision simply because of the nature of her pregnancy. In other words, better off to have the baby as soon as possible and be able to predict when the birth occurs rather than risk another false labor with Delia at home alone. This would be the best course of action to protect the health of the baby and mother.

So two days later on May 31st, I came home from work, took Delia by the hand and led her to the car. The drive to the hospital was routine and uneventful. It felt like we were going to a doctor's appointment rather than what I thought the drive to the hospital would be like on the day of our baby's birth. I pulled the car to a stop in the circular driveway for patient loading and had to conjure up excitement over the reality of the situation. I actually had to remind myself that despite how casual this all felt, the day had finally come. We were having a baby!

CHAPTER 3
THE BIG DAY

I dropped Delia off at the patient loading area at the hospital in Fremont with the agreement that we would meet inside at the admitting area. I perused the parking lot until I found a parking space. Naturally, all of the good spaces near the hospital were marked for doctors only. Eventually I found a space on the outer perimeter of the lot and started walking towards the large stucco structure of Washington Hospital. I walked into the glass foyer of the hospital and entered the admitting area where I saw Delia waiting in front of a large circular counter. Since everything had already been scheduled, we did not need to stop here and register. Instead we proceeded directly to a bank of elevators that were a short walk down a hallway to the left of the counter. We went up to the second floor, and the instant the elevator doors opened, there was no mistaking it: We were definitely in a hospital. We exited the elevator and went a short distance down a sterile white tile floor and white-walled hallway to the counter of a nurses' station. There was a distinct smell of Betadine and sterilizers in the air. As we approached the counter, a middle-aged nurse who seemed friendly but busy asked if she could help us. Delia gave her name to the nurse who then confirmed that they were expecting us. The nurse asked another slightly younger looking nurse if she could show us to our room. The other nurse agreed and told Delia that she would have to get into a wheelchair, gesturing towards several parked next to the nurses' station.

We were guided from the nurses' station to a room down the hall. It was a very stark, traditional looking hospital room compared to the homey atmosphere of today's birthing rooms.

There were oxygen and power outlets on the walls, monitoring equipment stuck in various parts of the room, and a large hospital bed with aluminum side railings plopped right in the middle. The bed had no end tables and about the only thing that was not completely utilitarian in the entire room was the television. I set my camera down on a small metal table in one corner of the room and looked at the clock on the wall, noticing it was 5:15 in the evening. I wondered how long we would have to be in this uninviting room.

Not much happened for the next several hours. Occasionally we were visited by nurses, and we filled out hoards of paper work. Then at around nine o'clock, a nurse came in and announced they were now going to administer a drug that would induce labor. The nurse wielded a large needle and poked it into Delia's arm. I watched the fluid from the needle get slowly pumped into Delia. It signaled a realization that Delia would be giving birth at any time now. Delia and I were filled with a nervous excitement. We knew that our lives would soon be changing forever. We were about to enter the world of parenthood.

My excitement started to wane and be replaced by exhaustion as the night went on. Delia went to sleep soon after the injection. I fought off sleep because I thought the birth was imminent, and I vowed to myself not to miss a thing. But as the minutes of waiting became hours, my resolve began to weaken. Starting at around one o'clock in the morning when the nurses made their rounds to check on Delia, I asked if I had time to step outside for a minute. Each time the nurses assured me that I could easily leave for a few minutes before anything happened. So I stepped outside to allow the cool night air to rejuvenate me long enough so that I could stay awake, at least until the next round. I sat on a bench outside the hospital and thought about the conversations that would soon transpire. *Guess what? We just had a seven pound, four ounce baby boy!*

The night droned on until finally at around five o'clock in the morning, approximately twelve hours after we checked into the hospital, Dr. Burns arrived. Dr. Burns, Delia's obstetrician, was an athletic looking woman about forty years old. She had a chiseled face and masculine mannerisms. We had met several times before during Delia's pregnancy, and she always maintained a professional and aloof demeanor. Dr. Burns began discussing Delia's condition with the nurses. Then they all briefly left the room. Shortly thereafter the nurses returned to administer to Delia another dose of the drug that would induce labor.

The additional shot made a significant difference. Now instead of sleeping, Delia was wide awake as her discomfort and labor pains increased considerably. I felt frustrated at my uselessness because after the second shot Delia started sweating and moaning with pain. I wanted to do something to help, but there was nothing I could do but stand at her side and try to comfort her. The nurses stepped up the frequency of their rounds and seemed to be monitoring more signs each time they did. I no longer asked about stepping outside.

But other than the elevation of Delia's discomfort, the second set of shots did not seem to be yielding any results. I watched as hour after hour Delia suffered in obvious pain and discomfort. At approximately ten o'clock in the morning, they broke her water hoping to speed up the process. Instead all it seemed to accomplish was put Delia in even more pain and discomfort. Time relentlessly continued to move on and nothing the nurses or Dr. Burns did seemed to change a thing. Delia continued to be in more pain with each tick of the clock.

At noon Dr. Burns succumbed to Delia's pleas for help and agreed to give her an epidural to help ease her pain. But at that point it seemed to be too little too late; she was sweating profusely and groaning with deep anguish each time a new labor pain would hit which was every few minutes now. Time refused to stop, and it was not her friend. Each minute seemed to bring with it new waves of pain. Delia would scream out, begging the nurses and doctor to do something. But they kept insisting it was not time yet. I watched trying fruitlessly for my words of encouragement to be of some comfort. I started to modify the imaginary conversations in my head. *Well, it was a little touch and go for a while there. But guess what? We just had a seven pound, four ounce baby boy!*

Finally, several more hours later, Delia was covered with sweat and letting out bloodcurdling screams from horrific pains that were almost nonstop. It became evident that now was the time that she was finally having our baby. I was holding one leg up and a nurse held the other leg. Dr. Burns was at the foot of the bed, and another nurse stood by. In one brief moment between contractions, Dr. Burns pointed out to me small black hairs attached to our baby's head that could now be seen. The excitement and joy of having the baby was mounting, and we were clearly very close.

"Okay now," she coached Delia, "you really have to push now."

Delia groaned with pain for what seemed like forever, but there was no change. And so naturally Delia allowed herself to relax again.

Dr. Burns ordered sternly, "Delia I know you're tired, but you really have to push now! Come on now . . . one more time!"

Delia screeched in pain, and I could hardly hold her leg as she gave a final push. Then, before my eyes, out came a little baby girl! Her skin looked light grey with large patches of skin that were black and blue, as if she were badly bruised. Her eyes were closed and her limbs seemed to hang still and lifeless. I assumed this was how all newborn babies looked. And so I felt happy and relieved. We have a baby girl, I thought; let the celebration begin!

The team of nurses and Dr. Burns quickly cut the baby's umbilical cord. The nurses took the baby over to a table at the foot of the bed while Dr. Burns stayed with Delia. I went to the table at the other corner of the room to get the camera.

What happened next continues to serve as a testimony to me of just how strong a woman my wife is. At 3:22 in the afternoon, nearly twenty-four hours after being admitted to the hospital, full of drugs and exhausted from more than ten hours of labor, my wife had the presence of mind to wonder about the baby.

Delia mumbled something, but it was unintelligible.

"What?" Dr. Burns asked.

"Why isn't my baby crying?" she mumbled with all of her remaining strength.

Her words were like a slap to my face that brought me out of my dreamy scripted happy moment of what I expected the birth to be like, into the reality of what was going on in the room at that moment. "Yeah," I thought to myself, "why isn't our baby crying?"

I now had the camera in hand and turned to approach the table where the baby was. I started snapping pictures of the baby because I was on automatic pilot and doing what I had planned for months to do at the birth. I quickly realized however that this was not a happy time to congratulate everyone on a successful delivery.

Instead the scene was more like that of an emergency room. The head nurse was barking out orders with authority and urgency. As Delia had aptly pointed out, our baby was not crying. What Delia did not know was that, in fact, she was not breathing either.

I watched in disbelief as our tiny little baby lay on a table surrounded by the two delivery nurses that worked desperately trying to resuscitate her. The head nurse said something, and the other nurse handed her what looked like a small oxygen mask with a black bag attached to it. The nurse fit the mask over the nose and mouth of our baby and they began pumping the bag. I was numb as I watched the nurse slowly squeeze the air from the bag into the lungs of our baby, and then release again. Time seemed to stand still as I watched in horror this effort to bring our daughter to life. Finally, after what seemed like forever, but was probably shortly after the C.P.R. began, our daughter let out a cry.

"Oh my God," I said, "she sounds like a cat!" I had no idea at the time how prophetic that statement would be.

The head nurse announced that the baby was breathing. But it was not said with a sense of joy and relief; it was more like a signal to the other nurse that now they could move on to the next phase of treatment. The intensity and urgency did not leave the room. Instead some type of machine was now hooked up to my daughter so that she could continue to breathe. More equipment was ordered, delivered to the room, and hooked up to the baby. The nurses then announced that they needed to take her to the nursery. I told Delia that I was going to stay with the baby. She mumbled her agreement.

I followed the procession of equipment, baby and hospital personnel down the hall to the nursery. Once we arrived at the nursery, the head nurse remained concerned and continued ordering the others around with authority. A young girl who looked like some type of nurses' assistant was standing with a clip board obviously filling out a form.

She innocently asked the head nurse, "How much does the baby weigh?"

The head nurse looked at her with disdain, like she was crazy to be asking about something so trivial at a time of life or death like this. "About five pounds!" she sneered before reverting back to telling the other people what they had to do.

The girl's face flushed with embarrassment as she marked her form and then left the room.

Finally, after several more minutes of intense and deliberate actions by the nursing team, our daughter was stabilized. She had tubes and monitors all over her body, but she had escaped the jaws of death.

I spent the next few hours shuffling back and forth from the nursery to Delia's room. Delia was pretty much delirious, but she appreciated the status reports. On one such visit to the room, there was a young woman who asked us if we had a name for the baby. Delia and I had agreed months before that if we had a girl we would combine the names of her grandmother and my sister and name her Montel Mercedes Evans. The woman asked if we were certain . . . that we could wait until the next morning if we would like to. Especially since it was such a traumatic birth, she did not want us to feel pressured. Delia and I insisted that we liked the name.

The medical emergency and trauma of Montel's birth seemed to calm down. However, our relief was short lived. On one of my stops at Delia's room, Dr. Burns entered and told us that our daughter was going to be moved to the children's hospital at Stanford University . . . that they were better equipped to handle a baby with these kinds of complications.

"But isn't she stable now?" Delia asked.

"Yes," Dr. Burns replied, "but her condition is still very fragile, and we don't really have the right type of equipment or personnel at this hospital." She seemed to be choosing her words very carefully, like there was something she knew that she did not want to tell us.

"Can I at least see my baby before you take her?" Delia pleaded.

Dr. Burns paused before she responded, "Well, okay I guess, but only for a minute."

So at a little after five o'clock in the evening, about two hours after she was born, a group of paramedics entered our room with a load of equipment in tow and Delia saw our daughter for the first time. They only let Delia see Montel for about two minutes before they insisted that for the baby's safety they transport her to Stanford right away. Once again we decided it best if I went with the baby.

I drove across the Bay to Lucile Packard Children's Hospital at Stanford University in Palo Alto. I entered the hospital and followed the signs to the neonatal intensive care unit (NICU). A pair of large stainless steel sinks was located outside of the doors to the unit. I approached the NICU, and the nurse receptionist informed me that I had to wash up before I could enter. I washed my hands thoroughly and then followed the nurse through the set of double doors.

We walked down an aisle of cribs in the dimly-lit room flanked by the most heart-breaking little babies I had ever seen. There were preemies that barely weighed more than a pound with fingers the size of match sticks. And there were babies that had obvious physical abnormalities. The babies were either in small plastic incubators called isolettes, or lay on radiant warmers; devices that resembled large padded square tables with the surface of the table able to be adjusted to different angles. All of the babies were hooked up to various machines and looked dreadfully exposed. They looked like something between human babies and fetuses as they lie motionless in their mechanical wombs. The nurse pointed to the radiant warmer at the end of the aisle on the right-hand side and said, "That one is your daughter."

Montel looked tiny and helpless. There were tubes, monitors, and IVs all over her body. She had two plastic oxygen tubes, one blue and another clear, that joined together and were taped to her mouth. The tubes were attached at the other end to some type of breathing apparatus. The machine pulsated in and out like an accordion. There were tubes attached to her feet, her hands, her stomach, and her heart. Several IV's dripped into her little body. There were monitors taped to her legs, her hands, and her heart. I stared at her and thought how sad for her to be introduced to this world in such a harsh and unloving way. It didn't seem fair for her. Instead of being in a world full of softness and cuddly love, she was lying exposed on a table with her legs and hands strapped down so that she could not move. And she was surrounded by massive amounts of equipment, monitors, and mechanical devices. Her eyes were closed and had some type of greasy gel smeared over them. Looking at her broke my heart. I felt so sad for this poor little baby.

I stood silently at the foot of her bed and sobbed. It was a pain like I had never experienced before in my life. It was not sadness, like when I found out that my grandmother died. Instead I was filled with a deep sorrow. It was a sorrow that emanated from my very soul. I was not even crying in a usual, weepy kind of way. I stood completely silent and motionless as the tears steadily flowed out of my eyes. I looked at my tiny newborn baby daughter strapped down flat on her back like some kind of perverted laboratory experiment, and I ached to hold her, to comfort her, to somehow make her world better. I desperately wished there was something that I could do for this tiny, ailing little baby girl . . . yet there was absolutely nothing that I could do to help. I had never felt more powerless in my life.

Eventually, I gave into my exhaustion and decided to go home. First though, I went back to Washington Hospital to see Delia again. I tried desperately to put the most upbeat spin possible on the circumstances. We talked for some time, and I tried my best to reassure her. Eventually Delia dropped off into sleep.

My thoughts shifted to the cruel irony of the situation. Across the Bay a little baby girl was strapped to her hospital bed looking like she needed so much love. And her exhausted mother lay here across the Bay in another hospital room, isolated from her. I got up to leave the hospital and went home thinking, "Thank God this day is over."

The big day . . . the day that I had been anxiously looking forward to for so long. The day I planned to call everyone I knew to announce the birth of our son. I had called only the closest of family and friends to explain the complications of our daughter. And so it went, on the day that I expected to be one of the happiest days of my life, I drove home alone and cried myself to sleep.

CHAPTER 4

DECISION

I woke up the next morning and called in to my work explaining the complications with my daughter. I then drove to Washington Hospital to visit Delia. When I walked into her room, she looked as though she had been waiting for me. All of her things were neatly stowed in bags, and she sat up and told me that she was checking out. I did not think it was a good idea because I thought it was too soon for her to be moving about. But I could tell by the look in her eye that nothing in this world could keep her from leaving that hospital to go visit her baby. So I lowered one of the aluminum railings of the bed and helped her as she gingerly rolled herself out of bed and into a waiting wheelchair. She was in obvious pain.

We signed some discharge papers at the nurses' station and made our way to the elevator. When the doors opened on the first floor, I pushed her wheelchair to the patient loading zone where she waited as I got the car. I stopped the car in the loading area, and she got out of the wheelchair very slowly and grimaced as she climbed into the car.

We drove toward Stanford to see our daughter, and one thing started becoming very clear to me . . . that while Delia's physical pain was substantial (and it was out of sheer stubbornness and determination that she was even with me), much greater was the emotional pain that she was feeling by being separated from her newborn daughter.

It may have been out of empathy for Delia, or it may have been that my thoughts were getting clearer now too, but as we continued our drive to Palo Alto, I began to feel more concern for the baby as well. After all, she looked so helpless the night before.

We arrived at the hospital, and I again placed Delia in a wheelchair before I parked the car and walked towards the hospital. Lucile Packard Children's Hospital was four or five stories tall; it was a modern looking beige stucco building with rust-orange colored windows, trim, and doors. I noticed for the first time the meticulous landscaped circular median in front of the hospital. The neatly trimmed grass and colorful flowers were accented with bushes that were trimmed in the shape of animals. There were bushes trimmed in the shape of a lion, an elephant with a bird riding on its back, and a giraffe. I thought the creatures seemed happy and carefree and while generally appropriate for children, they seemed cruelly out of place considering our daughter's circumstances and the stark room where she was now residing.

I pushed Delia to the intensive care unit where we washed our hands in the sink before being escorted by a nurse to Montel. When Delia saw Montel, it was like a wave of relief flowed over her. One would have never known that Montel was in intensive care and sustained by life support by the look on Delia's face. Her face lit up with pure love and joy as she gazed upon her newborn baby.

We continued to visit Montel over the next seven days as much as possible. Montel was moved into an isolette, and she wore a tiny felt sleeping mask covering her eyes. Her isolette was bathed in a yellow, special light to prevent her from getting jaundice. But, when we would ask the nurses if they knew anything more about her condition, they always said they wouldn't know anything until the tests came back from the lab. We would stand by her bedside holding each other and saying, "She'll be fine." It became our mantra. Leaving the hospital, we would pause at a long hallway just outside the neonatal intensive care unit to read letters of gratitude from parents and children survivors espousing their gratitude to the unit. One such letter was from a young woman who had survived against all odds and was now attending U.C. Davis. The hallway always served to give us hope that our daughter, like so many before her, would get through this troubling time in her life and be all right.

Nine days after Montel was born and admitted into intensive care, Delia and I were invited to meet with a counselor of the hospital. The whole time we drove to the hospital we continued reassuring each other, repeating many times our new favorite phrase, "She'll be fine."

Now waiting anxiously in a small sterile room, I was not so sure. After a few minutes of waiting, we were politely greeted by the counselor and introduced to a young woman who was one of the geneticists for the hospital. I felt an incredible amount of tension in the room. I can't recall exactly who said what. But we were told that Montel had a very rare genetic syndrome called Cri du Chat syndrome; that most people have forty-six chromosomes, but Montel has a portion of one of those chromosomes deleted, the short-arm of chromosome number five to be precise. I asked what that meant in terms of her prognosis.

The geneticist said, "I tried to find some information for you but all I could come up with was this." She plunked down an article from a medical journal. I don't remember a whole lot else that was said in the room that day. I remember Delia bursting into tears. I felt lightheaded and distant, as if I were hearing and watching the entire episode in a dream. In fact, I went into some form of shock and even went so far as to feel silly, and I remember making goofy and highly inappropriate jokes. And I remember their explaining to us that Montel could never do this, and never do that, and that we should consider putting her in an institution.

Once we left, I was completely preoccupied with learning more about Cri du Chat syndrome. We got home, and I started reading the medical journal article. I found out that *Cri du Chat* is French for *Cry of the Cat* because all babies with the syndrome, regardless of how small the chromosome deletion is, have a soft, high-pitched cry at birth that sounds similar to that of a cat. I recalled how I jokingly commented on Montel's cry at her birth, and my heart sank. I became engulfed by a deep sense of sorrow. A sorrow the depths of which I had only experienced a few times in my life, and I knew it was the type of hurt that would last for a long time, and one that I would never fully heal from.

I plugged away at the article and the diagnosis could not have been worse. When I reflect upon it now, I think nothing could have been more repulsive to me as a new parent than to read a medical journal that described our daughter like a scientific specimen, a human guinea pig, a thing, a thing that was flawed.

I read, "*A recent study by Wilkins et al. of sixty-five children with Cri du Chat syndrome reared in the home suggests that a much higher level of intellectual performance can be achieved than was previously suggested from studies performed on institutionalized patients. With early special schooling and a supportive home environment, some affected children attain the social and psychomotor level of a normal five to six year old.*" And, "*Cardiac abnormalities requiring frequent medical intervention during infancy and childhood were present in twenty-nine percent of patients with isolated deletion and fifty-five percent of those with unbalanced translocation.*" I trudged through page after page of language like, "*Physical growth was characterized by decreased height, poor weight gain, and significant microcephaly.*" I did not even know the meaning of the word "microcephaly."

As if the language was not bad enough, the cover page of the article had a large chart entitled, *Abnormalities*, with the word abnormalities bold and in capital letters. The chart was broken down into the following five categories: General, Performance, Craniofacial, Cardiac, and Hands. Each category had a list of more detailed symptoms and a percentage of those children with Cri du Chat syndrome who had the "abnormality." I kept feeling more desperate as I struggled to find some sense of hope. But the further I studied, the more the severity of the syndrome was revealed to me. For example, under the category of Performance, 100% had mental deficiency and 78% had hypotonia. I did not know what "hypotonia" meant either. In fact, I had to learn a whole list of medical terms that day:

Hypotonia – state of being hypotonic.

Hypotonic – having deficient muscle tone or tension.

Microcephaly – condition of abnormal smallness of the head usually associated with mental defect.

Epicanthal folds – a prolongation of a fold of the skin of the upper eyelid over the inner angle or both angles of the eye. Called also "Mongolian fold."

Phenotypic – the visible properties of an organism that are produced by the interactions of the genotype and the environment.

Once I finished reading the article, I realized that Cri du Chat syndrome, the syndrome that our daughter had, was very grave. I was absolutely devastated. Every last flicker of hope was doused by the reality of knowing that even if she did make it through a whole litany of physical and medical problems, she would still be severely mentally retarded. This meant that she would have an IQ between twenty and forty. On a bell curve of ranges of human intelligence she would be at the far left-hand tail of the curve and be in the lowest .13 *percent*. I started visualizing what it would be like to walk down a long line of ten thousand people, ten thousand people lined up and ranked by intelligence: In the front would be the best and the brightest, and then, after walking past literally thousands of people, in the very back, somewhere statistically amongst the last thirteen would be our daughter. In fact, even among the population of people with mental retardation, she would fall into the lowest 4 – 6%. I could not imagine anything that would have made the diagnosis worse.

Although in shock, I immediately started considering what we needed to do. We could let her go, sever all ties to her I thought. After all, there were probably experts that would be better at taking care of this type of person. Besides, this child sounded like she was going to be a real burden, a burden that I was not sure that I was prepared to undertake. Delia and I started doing a little dance . . . I quit going to the hospital to visit our daughter from that moment on, and she pretended not to notice.

For the next several days, I talked to family and friends, soliciting advice on what they thought we should do. I think my inquiries must have projected my bias towards giving her up for adoption or putting her in an institution and moving on because the responses varied from completely non-committal to absolutely agreeing that the sensible thing to do was give her up totally. No one I talked to strongly argued the position that we should keep her.

Dan, a good friend of mine, asked me if I was Catholic. I told him that I was raised Catholic, but that I hadn't been to church for years. "Well," he said, "since you're Catholic why don't you call a priest?" He completely ignored my disclaimer of how long it had been since I went to church. I told him that I might do that. But I secretly thought to myself what a ridiculous idea it was. Of course I knew what a priest would say – *Keep that baby no matter what - even if she makes you miserable for the remainder of your life - it is your duty. You shouldn't be so worried about this life anyway, focus on the next life.*

I continued talking to people for the next several days. All of my coworkers and friends were either silent or thought that we should not keep our daughter.

I remember one morning having coffee with Carl, a portfolio manager where I worked, to find out his opinion of what I should do. Carl was good looking, wore expensive suits, drove a BMW, and was the picture of success, confidence, and power. I looked up to Carl and respected his opinion. After explaining the circumstances to him, Carl was very practical and agreed with what was starting to become my conclusion too. Based upon the severity of the syndrome, we were better off without that girl. And the girl would probably be better off with someone other than us too. He recommended that we give her up for adoption.

I also remember Jane, a very prim and proper grandmotherly-type woman, who held the same level of accounting position in the company that I did. I knew Jane was somewhat religious, and she always seemed a little tense to me. It was a small office, so I knew she was aware of the decision I was trying to make. Yet she conspicuously fell silent whenever a discussion about my daughter came up. That gave me a gut feeling that she thought we should keep our daughter.

I continued to grapple with what to do for several more days but had a pretty good idea that we should give up our daughter. It had now been a week since we received the diagnosis, and for me the only real decision left to make was whether we should give our daughter up for adoption or put her in a good institution.

In the meantime, Delia had been visiting our daughter everyday.

It seemed like a good time to have a talk. So I waited for Delia to get home from the hospital, and we sat down at the kitchen table. I knew Delia was a reasonable person and that she would be able to see what was clearly best for everyone.

I explained that in my opinion we had to be practical and do what was best for the baby. We should let someone who was inclined to take care of people like that take care of our daughter. She was going to be too much for us to be able to handle.

Delia completely disagreed. "She is our daughter, and we should take care of her no matter what."

"Look," I said, "all that I'm saying is the baby's quality of life will be better at a facility, or with a family that is equipped to handle people like that. I admit it . . . I don't think that I can handle it."

"I think people can handle whatever life gives them," Delia said.

"What if we want other children," I said. "It won't be fair to them. We will need to spend all of our time with this one."

"I think you should accept responsibility for the child you have before you start worrying about the children you don't have," Delia retorted.

We argued back and forth, and we continued to get angrier. We were each getting frustrated once we realized that neither one of us was going to be able to easily persuade the other. If anything, our two points of view were getting hardened. The argument escalated until we were screaming at each other.

Finally, Delia broke down and started crying. She looked defeated and exasperated realizing that I was never going to see things her way. "It is your own daughter for God's sake!" she said to herself as much as to me through her sobs. "You never even call her by her name. Why don't you ever call her by her name?"

"*Why don't I call her by her name?*" I was stunned. I now realized how deep and wide the chasm of our different perspectives was, and it made me realize the futility of continuing this discussion. I turned and walked away. I walked outside and stood on our front porch. "*Why don't I call her by her name?*" Her words kept cycling through my head. My God, didn't she read the medical journal? "*Why don't I call her by her name?*" Delia really doesn't get it at all I thought; this is not really a person . . . this creature is one notch above a vegetable, with arms and legs. This is a person who will *never* work, *never* live independently, and probably *never* even talk. I mean for all practical purposes she would literally be better off dead.

I felt so hurt and angry about the situation. Hurt and angry that there was nothing that we could do to change the way our daughter was born. But also hurt and angry that Delia was being so irrational, acting as if we had some kind of obligation to take this baby home. I thought that while it was obviously really bad luck, we should cut our losses and move on. I didn't understand why we had to make the bad luck into a life sentence of caring for this thing that lay in the hospital across the Bay.

The next day I wanted someone to reaffirm my position. So late that evening, I called my friend Dan again, and again he suggested that I talk to a priest. I hung up the phone and decided to call all of the Catholic churches in the phone book just so that if he suggested it again I could tell him that I had tried to talk to a priest, and it didn't work. It was ten o'clock at night on a weekday, so I really did not expect to reach anyone as I started systematically calling each of the Catholic churches listed in the phone book. The first few were as I had expected: they either rang off the hook, or I got an answering machine. Then I called one, and a real live human being answered the phone on the other end.

"Hello," said a very elderly man's voice on the other end.

"Uh . . . hello," I stammered. "I'm uh . . . I'm looking for a priest."

"I'm a priest," the voice said.

I couldn't believe it! I thought, "What priest answers the phone at ten o'clock at night?" I managed to compose myself and explain the circumstances of our daughter. Then I listened, sure that I would be receiving a self-righteous lecture on how I had to take our daughter home or I would go straight to where there was fire and brimstone.

The priest said, "Boy, that's a tough one all right. I'm not sure what you should do. It really is up to you though. I'll talk to you as long as you like and try to help you as best I can, but ultimately it's your decision."

I was shocked. This was not the automatic answer I expected. What struck me most as we continued talking was not so much what he said but how he said it. He sounded concerned and sincere. He was a concerned friend, not a self-righteous religious cleric. We talked for several more minutes. At one point I was explaining how I rationalized that since our daughter was revived by the nurses at the time of her birth her life was not really meant to be in the first place.

"So," I said, "It was not God's will for her to even be here."

"Oh no," he corrected, "I know those medical people are good . . . but believe me, they are not miracle workers. If God did not want her to be alive she would not be alive."

As soon as I heard them, I knew his words were true. We talked longer, and then, when we ended our conversation, he wished the best for me. And I sensed that he really meant it. Unlike my initial expectations, he was not judgmental or condescending at all.

A few days later, I met with Susan, a property manager of a large apartment complex which was one of the complexes that I oversaw the accounting for. I sat in her office, and we ended up discussing my daughter. Susan revealed to me that her boyfriend had an autistic son who lived in an institution up in Alaska. She reassured me that I was definitely doing the right thing. Susan told me that I should try to talk some sense into Delia . . . that if Delia were smart, she would quit seeing the baby and try to get over this as quickly as possible. Just forget that the baby was ever born and move on. Otherwise, this would become an ongoing nightmare that would never end and would consume our entire lives. I completely agreed. I was no longer on the fence; my decision was made. Susan was right. It may seem selfish I thought, but I felt I had every right to reject the destiny of being saddled by such a needy person. It was a tremendous relief to finally come to a solid decision. And I knew it was a decision I could live with. After all, I did not volunteer for this.

Now that my decision was made, my only concern was how Delia would react . . . I knew that it might cause the breakup of our marriage. But I felt that I had no choice. There was no way I was going to get stuck with such a burdensome child. I went home that night and told Delia firmly, yet as gently as possible, that my mind was made up, that I would never again have anything to do with our daughter. We went to bed and, for the first time that I remember in our relationship, we lay down in bed together without speaking a word. I was not sure if she planned on leaving me or not. But it didn't matter; regardless of the outcome, I had made my decision.

The next day at work I received a call from Delia. She said that she was at the hospital and that the baby was being released. She said that she had thought about it and would go along with an adoption for our daughter. Her logic was simple: A child with this severe a disability would be difficult under the best of circumstances and virtually impossible to take care of as a single mother.

So, eighteen days after her birth and nine days after her diagnosis, my daughter was ready to be released from the hospital. Delia asked me to take them to the foster home where my daughter would stay until an adoption was made. I sensed that the idea of my picking both of them up was my wife's ploy, so that I would see my daughter again and upon doing so would change my mind about the adoption. I agreed to pick them up because I am a very stubborn man and I knew that nothing was going to change my mind on this. So, with a strong resolve that adoption was for the best, I headed to the hospital.

My wife and daughter met me in a basement room of the hospital. Apparently my daughter had graduated from intensive care to intermediate care. Delia was sitting on a couch feeding her a bottle. Our daughter was so small that her arms were barely longer than Delia's hands. But her color looked better and she was dressed in a cute little white baby outfit with feet sewn into it. She even had a white bandana with pink flowers on it. But her eyes had obviously still not opened, and her hips and feet looked awkward and malformed. Her face looked strange and moon shaped with eyes that were wide apart. It reminded me of the syndrome and the business at hand. So, after taking a few pictures, I suggested that it was time to go.

We left the hospital, and drove across the Bay to the foster home near where we lived in the East Bay. At the foster home, we went inside to meet our daughter's temporary caretakers. I was struck by two things at the home. First, how many children they had. It may sound ridiculous, but I somehow envisioned that our daughter's caretakers would be people who had been sitting around their entire lives waiting for our daughter. I imagined it would be their destiny or something. To the contrary, these people had around six special needs children; four that they had adopted and two foster children. They were in the business of taking in special needs kids.

The other thing that struck me about the house was how incredibly ordinary it seemed. There were no special ramps, extra wide doors, or anything else to indicate that there were special needs people here. It was just a regular house with a whole bunch of kids.

Everything went well until right before we were going to leave. They asked us if we would pray with them. We agreed, and they proceeded to pray a heartfelt prayer for the well-being of our daughter. When we had finished, I began to feel a little guilty and I questioned myself, asking myself if my decision was truly based on what was best for my daughter or based on selfishness. But, I remembered the commitment I had made earlier to myself, and we said our good-byes.

Then, as my wife and I were driving silently towards a restaurant we planned to go to for dinner that night, I started having doubts. I was thinking about what my daughter would say to me if she could ever have the ability to talk: "I'm sorry Daddy. I can't help the way I am. Why are you dumping me? I'm sorry I'm not good enough for you. What did I do to deserve being abandoned?" And the words her foster parents had prayed: "May God bless this little girl and protect her from harm. Please let this vulnerable little girl find love and protection. All this girl needs, Lord, is love." These thoughts clashed with thoughts of the logical, rational conversations I had had with numerous people concluding I did not want to be burdened with a child like this: "I don't want to be changing my thirteen-year-old daughter's diaper someday. What if we have other kids; it wouldn't be fair to them. The people that adopt these kids are experts. They can take better care of her than we can." To take my mind off this internal conflict, I turned on the radio. A sad Country and Western song was playing that talked about children playing and said that we are all seeds in the hands of God or something like that. I quickly turned the radio back off. But the conflict raging inside of me could not be turned off so easily.

We went to dinner, but it felt like a part of us was missing. I couldn't understand it. We had *never* had our daughter with us since she was born. How could something be missing that you never had? I guess when she was lying in a hospital bed somehow she was still ours. Now in a foster home it was different. Then there was her room. The cute little baby room that we had spent so much time and care in making had *never* been occupied and I had never given it a second thought. Now however, I couldn't stop thinking about that room, the *Kelley's Kite* bedding on the crib, the mobile of small kites, the matching light pine-colored dresser, changing table, rocking chair, and crib. The same room that represented so much joy and hope now seemed very empty and sad.

I kept trying to remember all of the perfectly sound reasoning and logic that had formulated my decision. But what was happening had nothing to do with reasoning and logic. It was more like a gut feeling. A gut feeling that said giving our daughter up for adoption was wrong. That no matter how hard I pretended otherwise, there was nothing special about those foster parents that just took her in. And there would be nothing special about the people that ended up adopting her either. They were just ordinary people. Ordinary people that were willing to love our daughter the way she was.

By the time our dessert arrived, I decided to trust the gut feelings.

"We should go back and get her," I said to Delia.

"What?" Delia asked, but by the excitement in her voice

she had obviously heard me.

"We should go back and get her," I said again.

"We can't," she said, "It's too late. They already have her."

"They can't stop us; she *is* our daughter." I said. "In other words, I think you were right; I think it is the right thing to do. So let's go back and get her."

We left without eating dessert. We drove to the home where we had just left our daughter a few hours before, picked her up from a surprised set of foster parents, and then we all went home.

Delia told me later that it was the happiest moment of her life.

CHAPTER 5
ACCEPTANCE

We took Montel home, but that did not mean all was well. My feelings were dreadfully torn. On one hand, I wanted so badly to be a typical joyful parent with our newborn baby. And in many ways she was perfectly normal. She was awfully cute, with dark hair that covered her tiny head, golden brown skin, and tiny hands and feet. She was such a tiny little thing, not even big enough to hold herself up. But on the other hand, I was struggling with the reality of our daughter's disability. She was extraordinarily docile for a newborn baby, and her eyes were always only half-opened even when she was fully awake. I felt terribly sorry for her.

For one thing, I had not been around people with disabilities much at all in my entire life. The only person in my life I could even think of who had a disability was a neighborhood boy named Mark who lived across the street from me for about two years when I was growing up. I remember that Mark behaved like a small child even though he was around thirteen years old.

Mark had an obsession with Batman. I remember Mark often wore a Batman costume: gray tights, black fitted shorts, a gray spandex material shirt with the black batman logo on the chest and a black cape. He topped it off with a black mask complete with pointed ears. He would run around the neighborhood dressed in his Batman costume humming and singing the Batman show's theme song: "Na-na-na-na, na-na-na-na, Batman!" I remember he was often taunted by the other kids in the neighborhood.

"Batman isn't real, Stupid!"

"Yes he is," Mark would say back. "I even know where

his cave is, so who's stupid now?"

"Oh right! So where do you think his cave is . . . Stupid!"

Mark would lean in and talk quietly so as not to reveal his secret too loudly, lest the Joker, Cat Woman or another nemesis of his hero should overhear. "His cave is in the basement of Fairdale School."

Fairdale was the local neighborhood elementary school, about three blocks away from where we lived.

"Oh right!" his interrogator would say, howling with laughter, "You're so stupid! Like I said before . . . Batman isn't real!"

Perhaps others would join in, or the original teaser would just keep up a relentless verbal attack; but eventually Mark would go running home in tears with his hands covering his ears yelling, "Batman is real!. . . I'm not stupid! . . . Batman is real! . . ."

The especially sad aspect of this teasing is that often the perpetrator or perpetrators were half his age and size. But Mark just didn't have the emotional or mental maturity to be able to stand up to them.

I remember one time a group of about ten neighborhood kids were chasing him and taunting him with rocks and sticks. I can honestly say that I was not a participant in the exercise. However, I didn't go to any great lengths to stop the harassment either. I followed along with the mob as it proceeded down the street in front of several houses and watched with morbid curiosity as Mark got poked and hit while the group of children chanted, "Ignorant!" At one point Mark said something that made the leader of his tormentors modify the chant to, "Ignorant! You're getting a little smarter...Ignorant!" I remember how the group cruelly laughed. Eventually Mark was cornered in a driveway where an adult neighbor intervened, breaking up the group. And even though I never participated in that, or the routine teasing and torturing of Mark, I do remember that he was the laughing stock of the neighborhood.

To think of having a child like Mark made me feel ashamed and embarrassed. Then I would turn around and feel guilty about feeling ashamed and embarrassed.

Another reason I struggled with Montel's disability was because of my own ideas about quality of life. I thought there were certain requirements that made life worth living. I was not sure exactly what those requirements were, but I was certain that Montel's disability crossed the line. In other words, I felt that if I were to get involved in an accident or somehow I were to be left as severely disabled as her syndrome was going to make her, I would rather be dead. I projected these feelings onto her and assumed that if she had the choice she would prefer to be dead as well.

So early on I made a deliberate effort to avoid getting too emotionally attached to Montel. And I would literally pray every night that she would die. This was not as mean-spirited and cold as it may sound. Actually it was more like praying for a mercy killing. "Dear Heavenly Father, please spare my daughter from a life of ridicule and humiliation. If it were just her body I could understand it Lord. But it is her mind. She will never be able to think for herself, have a relationship with a man or do any of the normal things that make life worth living. So please Lord, please spare her, and all of us, from continuing this façade of a so-called life. Let her pass on Lord, let it be as painless as possible, but Lord I beg you, let her pass on."

I just could not help it. No matter how I looked at it, I thought she had such major quality of life issues that she really would be better off dead. Therefore, I tried to maintain an emotional detachment to make it easier in the event my prayers were ever answered.

It was fairly easy to stay detached the first six weeks that she was home because Delia was still on maternity leave. But when Delia returned to work, I started taking care of Montel at night while Delia was at work, and it became more difficult. I made sure that all of the essentials were covered: Her diapers got changed, she got fed, and I would even start the mechanical swing so as to keep her relatively content. But I did everything mechanically and with a concerted effort to maintain my aloofness . . . just in case. In those early days, Montel was an extremely docile baby which aided in my effort to keep her at an emotional distance.

But about three weeks after Delia returned to work, when Montel was about eleven weeks old, I had her outside, and a slight breeze was blowing her hair. She opened her eyes and smiled at me! I couldn't believe it . . . it was the first sign of emotion that she had shown at all in her entire life . . . and it was directed at me! I held her up towards the wind again, and she smiled again. I felt so special holding her, not only because I was the one to whom she exhibited emotion for the first time, but because it felt so *normal.* For a moment I was able to forget about what I perceived to be the dreary life she had before her and just be her Dad. Just feel joy in the fact that she felt joy.

Montel started showing more signs of personality. She started smiling more; she even laughed sometimes, and so instead of winding up the mechanical swing, I spent more and more nights rocking her to sleep in my arms. Time moved on . . . and I could not help myself . . . despite my best efforts to keep her at an emotional distance, I was falling in love. The problem was the more affection I felt for her, the more acute my pain was when I considered what I perceived to be her dismal life. And so I would double-up my efforts to keep her away. I would never have done anything bad to Montel; the point is that I had settled into a routine of maintaining an unnatural distance from her. I was more like a well-trained robot taking care of her basic needs than I was a father.

Well, it is said that God works in mysterious ways . . . and I for one believe it. One evening while Delia was at work, and I was watching Montel, I put Montel in the swing until she fell asleep and I gingerly moved her to her crib.

After I put her to bed, I went to the living room, sat down

on our sofa, and started watching Monday Night Football. The ball was kicked off and the running back who caught the ball for the receiving team ran it back all the way for a touchdown. I couldn't believe it. It was the third touchdown the same back had scored that game! He was having an incredible night. Strangely, once he was in the end-zone, instead of doing the usual celebration, he seemed a little distracted and scanned the fans looking for someone. As his teammates joined him in the end-zone giving him high-fives and congratulating him, he responded with high-fives and thanks, but in a sort of cursory manner; he was still obviously looking for someone in the crowd. Then, finally his eyes lit up, and he quickly ran over to a section of the end-zone where he jumped up and handed the ball to a fan. It was a young boy in a wheelchair. The announcers fell silent. The camera showed the young boy hunched over in his wheelchair holding the ball in his crumpled arms with a look of pure joy on his face. It was so sweet. Finally one of the announcers said in a thoughtful tone, "You know they fine guys in the NFL for doing that . . . but if ever there should be an exception to that rule, this is it."

And then it hit me. Here was a professional athlete, the epitome of athleticism, endurance, and physical perfection, and he subjected himself to a possible fine so that he could acknowledge the value of this little boy with special needs. In the meantime, here I sit, a middle-aged couch potato, and I can't even acknowledge the value of my own daughter in the other room. I had never felt more ashamed, and I realized then I had to change.

But how? My prejudice and fear had been built over an entire lifetime. How could I make it just go away? That night instead of praying my usual prayer to save Montel and take her life, I prayed that I might find a way to accept her.

My prayers were answered, somewhat. Over the next several months, Montel started showing a lot of personality and progress, and I was able to start accepting her. Well, I considered it acceptance at the time, but it was really more of a denial. I became convinced that the diagnosis was in error and that there was nothing really wrong with her; or that only some of the cells had the deletion, a condition known as mosaic, meaning that the long term prognosis would be much more difficult to predict and would depend upon how many cells had the deletion.

But whatever the reason, there was no holding back now. In the evenings when I was alone with her, I showered her with my love. I read books to her and took her for walks in the stroller while I talked to her. I rocked her to sleep every night to country and western music. I swore it was her favorite kind of music and, you guessed it, mine too!

I would start with songs that had a lively beat. I would cradle her in my arms and rock her with each beat. The more active the better; she would smile up at me and laugh when I turned up the beat or swung her high into the air and then back down again. After a few minutes, we would switch to slow songs. She would settle down and relax in my arms, closing her eyes as I swayed her to the music. But she still insisted upon being rocked. If I stopped she would open her eyes and if I waited too long to start the motion up again she would even start crying. But eventually she would fall off into a sound sleep. I would kiss her and gently tuck her into her crib.

In the meantime, in November, Delia and I found out that she was pregnant again. We both felt a mixture of excitement and terror about having another baby. We had planned on eventually having another one . . . but we feared the prospect of having another child with a disability. One thing that made it more bearable was the fact that I continued to get more convinced all the time that the problems with Montel had been exaggerated. She continued to show signs of progress. And each little sign of progress that she made was not just another milestone . . . but hope that the original diagnosis was wrong.

My optimism was infectious, and Delia started noting things that Montel did that seemed too advanced for a Cri du Chat baby as well. She was trying to stand up by herself, crawling all around by herself, and even making sounds like she was trying to talk. By March, when Montel was nine months old, we were so convinced that she was either normal or mosaic that we insisted on getting a second opinion.

I met Delia at Oakland Children's Hospital during my lunch hour. We walked into the doctor's office and waited for him to join us and give us the results of the second blood test. We nervously sat in the room hoping that as we suspected there had been a terrible mistake, and Montel was normal. Instead the doctor confirmed that Montel had Cri du Chat syndrome. Trying to maintain some flicker of hope, I asked if she would ever be able to live independently. You see over the last few months, I had plenty of time to grapple with what criteria determined if quality of life was so impaired that it was no longer worth living. And for me that litmus test was whether or not one could live independently.

"No," the doctor said, "she will probably never be able to live independently."

We asked more questions, but most of the answers we already knew. The bottom line was that she had the syndrome. And we knew every horrific ramification of that fact.

The doctor asked me, "So, how do you feel?"

"I am back to where I was last June," I said candidly. "I wish we never brought her home. I wish we had given her up for adoption or put her in an institution."

I went back to work and managed to block out the bad news from the hospital. But when I went home that night, I knew I was not all right. Due to the change of heart that I had the autumn before, I knew that I must somehow learn to accept my daughter. But once again I had no idea of how to do that. So that night, feeling as if it was even more hopeless than ever, I again prayed for the ability to accept her.

The next day at work I got very angry with one of the staff accountants who worked for me about something he had done. He made a careless mistake and, in my opinion, he should have known better. Anyway, I angrily snapped at him, and I knew that I had better leave for a moment to cool down before I said or did something that I would regret. So I headed down a set of stairs, followed by a long hallway, through a door. The door swung out onto the ground level employee parking lot.

I was standing in the parking lot getting some fresh air when I noticed a pleasant looking, dark-haired young woman approaching, walking on the sidewalk next to the parking lot. She was carrying a cardboard pet carrier.

"Hi," she said. "I have a kitten in here." She sounded very friendly and had a certain innocent quality about her.

"That's nice," I told her.

"His name is Jax," she said. And I realized that even though she was probably twenty something years old, her mannerisms and speech sounded more like that of a child.

"What a cute name," I said, hoping that I didn't sound too patronizing.

She said, "I had to take the fifty-seven and transfer to the eighty-eight to get Jax to the vet."

"Well good for you," I said. "Do you live around here?"

"Yeah, I live in a home over there," she said, pointing up the street to a house that my coworkers had warned me to stay away from because it housed a group of disabled people who would bother you by pan-handling if you came near them. "They said I can't keep Jax unless he has his shots."

We talked some more about how she found Jax, what a fine-looking kitten it was, and how she had always wanted a kitten growing up. After a few minutes she said, "Well, good-bye; it was real nice talking to you."

I felt relaxed and soothed from our pleasant little chat. I started walking back into the office reflecting upon how cute it was that she loved that kitten so much, and how she was so proud of herself for accomplishing the simple feat of making it to the veterinarian and back. I thought to myself, "I wouldn't mind if Montel were like that someday."

Then I stopped cold in my tracks. I heard somewhere that only God can change your heart, and the thought gave me chills. Because I realized that in that split second - in an instant - the indifference and callousness towards people with disabilities that had taken literally an entire lifetime for me to form had just been dissolved in a flash. After all, the girl that I had just spoken to, the girl that I had conceded I wouldn't mind if Montel turned out like, was obviously too mentally diminished to live independently. So much for my litmus test.

I felt at peace with myself for the first time in months. I had a warm feeling deep down inside and now had a new perspective about Montel, and her disability. Instead of feeling sorry for myself and wondering how this could happen to me, I now felt really special that God had entrusted me to take care of this very special person. I was flattered to have been chosen for this special assignment, and I vowed to do my best to be worthy of His endorsement. The change was permanent too; from that day forward my acceptance of Montel was unflappable.

There simply are not words that can adequately explain what happened to me that day. But all I can say is that it completely and immediately changed my heart. God in a very loving and gentle way had answered my prayer. Because from that split second on, I somehow knew, knew with every fiber of my being, three basic truths.

One, God was in charge. I didn't need to try to figure out everything in the universe. It was not by *coincidence* that on that day, the day after I prayed for acceptance of my daughter, a mentally retarded woman crossed my path. It was the only time that I saw a person with a mental disability like that for years before, and for years after.

Two, Montel was given to us for a reason. I might never know what that reason was, at least in this lifetime. But it was not an accident. We were meant to have her.

And three, I knew that the reason was good. We did not have Montel to punish me or Delia, and certainly it was not to punish Montel. No, I knew that there was a higher purpose for Montel's life. And while it is true that every child is God's child, it was especially true with Montel. I was merely given the opportunity to be her earthly father.

So on that warm sunny spring day, I had a complete change of heart. My prayers were answered. Finally, I was able to let go, trust God, and accept Montel, disability and all.

CHAPTER 6
SMALL MIRACLES

The entire first year of Montel's life seemed full of conflicting emotions and drama. There was the shock of her diagnosis, followed by the agonizing decision of whether or not to take her home, and the first few months of her at home with my pushing her away emotionally. Then an artificial acceptance . . . an acceptance rooted in denial that there was anything wrong with her at all, and the crushing reality that she had the syndrome, and the severity of that syndrome. And finally complete acceptance.

As if all of that was not enough going on in my life, I started attending graduate school that winter because I wanted to make a career change from accounting to information technology (IT). This was back in the day when smaller companies like the one I was working for did not have formal IT departments. Instead they had an IT guru. To be an IT guru one had to know barely more than anyone else in the office about computer systems. I had become the IT guru for our company, and I liked it. In fact, I liked it better than the accounting work that was my primary function; thus the motivation to go back to school and change careers.

There were so many emotional highs and lows that year. In late March of that year, about a week after we received the devastating second diagnosis confirming Montel's syndrome, Delia and I were in one of the patient rooms of Dr. Burns' office. At the time Delia was around five months pregnant, and Dr. Burns wanted to give us the results of the amniocentesis that she had performed to make sure there were no genetic abnormalities with this baby. We were hugely relieved to find out that there were no obvious genetic problems, like Down syndrome or of course Cri du Chat syndrome.

Then Dr. Burns asked, "Do you want to know the sex of the baby too?"

Delia and I looked at each other and knew exactly where we stood on this one. I answered for both of us: "We want to know the sex, hair color, eye color, S.A.T. scores, favorite foods, anything at all that you can tell us. We had enough surprises with the first one to last us a lifetime!"

Dr. Burns laughed and said, "You're having a boy."

It felt really strange . . . I remembered how we originally thought we were having a boy when we had Montel. Now I knew with utter certainty that we were expecting a boy. And yet I felt less sure of the outcome than I had felt with the first one. I was so worried deep down that something would be wrong again. I just nervously hoped with all my heart that he would be healthy.

A few months later, just when we thought things were finally settling down, on May 13th, I got a call from my Aunt Doris, my favorite aunt, who lived in Hayward. She had just suffered an aneurism and was in the hospital. Still in graduate school and very busy, I saw her every night and weekend, spending as much time with her as possible. In only a few days, on May 26th, she died. I truly loved my Aunt Doris and was deeply saddened by her loss. And so the emotional rollercoaster continued up to, and even beyond Montel's first birthday, June 1st. I was mourning my aunt and joyfully anticipating the birth of my son at the same time.

Then at two o'clock in the morning on August 1st, Delia went into labor. I nervously drove to Washington Hospital, not missing the irony that this was how I expected the drive to the hospital for the first baby's birth to be.

We checked into the hospital, and we noticed that the rooms had been completely refurbished. The room was inviting and homey. The décor was like a country style home with cute wallpaper, attractive wooden night stands, table and chairs, and even a large lounge chair for me to sleep in if necessary.

Shortly after arriving in the room, Delia asked one of the nurses if she could have an epidural. A stocky nurse calmly checked to see how much Delia was dilated. The nurse examined Delia and suddenly looked up with a surprised expression on her face and said, "Nine centimeters. I'm sorry honey; it's too late for an epidural. You're having this baby!"

The nurse rushed out of the room to call Dr. Burns. Dr. Burns arrived shortly thereafter. Then Delia's labor pains began in earnest, and Dr. Burns coached her on breathing and pushing while a nurse held one of Delia's legs and I held the other.

At 4:54 A.M., not even three hours after arriving at the hospital, Sean Casey Evans was born. No need for Delia to wonder about this one. He immediately was letting out cries that could be heard in five counties. It was the most beautiful sound on earth. I was excited and happy, but at the same time I kept questioning the nurses and Dr. Burns if he was all right. I counted ten fingers and ten toes . . . which was a good sign.

Throughout the morning, the nurses and Dr. Burns kept trying to reassure me that everything was fine . . . that I should relax and enjoy the baby. In other words, I should react more like a typical parent of a newborn, as I had planned for months to react when our first baby was born. But by now with Montel's birth, I had become aware of many different types of disabilities, and I could not stop worrying. I thought, "What if he is autistic? There is no way we would know that until he is older." So, even though there was no indication otherwise, I just kept hoping and praying that he was healthy and normal.

We took Sean home, and it did not take long at all for us to see the difference between the two babies' development. Sean rolled over sooner, sat up sooner, cruised around the furniture sooner. And he was always much more alert and displayed much more personality than Montel when she was at the same age. Yes, there was no doubt that he was developing normally. And he added a new and refreshing dimension to our family.

Of course we still loved Montel with all of our hearts, but Sean somehow added a much healthier perspective to the whole thing. We no longer dwelled on Montel and especially on her disability. We went from having a daughter with a disability, to being a family with two children; and incidentally one of the children had a disability.

As years passed, I began to realize that Montel had a very subtle yet profound quality about her. There was something very spiritual or even kind of mystical about her.

For example, some time in the fall of the year she was born, during my "denial period," I told Delia about the time I called the priest when Montel was first born. Delia was fascinated by the story and one thing led to another until we decided to go to that church one Sunday.

We arrived at a Spanish style church that had a red tile roof and white stucco walls. Inside the church were colorful stained glass windows, and high above the altar, large dull silver pipes of varying lengths protruded up from the pipe organ below. The church had an aroma that was a mixture of elderly woman perfume, old wooden pews, and burning incense; it was delightful yet musty at the same time. We discovered later that it was one of the oldest churches in California, dating back to the middle nineteenth century.

We sat at the end of an aisle with Montel between us. As the service began, a procession of altar boys and a very old priest entered the central aisle of the church and passed right next to the pew where we were seated. I got excited and whispered to Delia that the priest was probably the one I had talked to because he seemed very old just as the voice sounded to me on the phone that night.

It was the first time I had been to church as an adult. It was familiar, yet strangely much different from what I had expected. As the service continued, I was amazed that even though I had not been to church for so long, I remembered everything. I knew when to sit, when to stand, when to kneel, and what to say. Nothing had changed. Except for me, that is. The prayers and values now had such a deeper meaning to me as an adult. It forced me to confront the fact that most of my core values had been formed in a church very similar to this one. Sitting in the pew and watching the old priest perform the service made me appreciate the traditions of the Catholic Church as I never had before. I was captivated by the service as I pondered how these same rituals had been performed for hundreds, in fact, thousands of years.

At this point I should probably interject that at this time Montel looked liked a perfectly normal baby. Other than a close inspection by a person who knew what to look for, no one could tell that she had any kind of genetic syndrome.

Anyway, the mass ended, and the altar boys led the procession once again down the center aisle, only this time heading out of the church. They all walked slowly past our aisle. When the priest passed the pew where we were sitting, he suddenly stopped, took a half step back and looked over at Montel. He grabbed Montel's hand and looked her in the eye and paused for a moment. Then he looked over at Delia and gently patted her shoulder. Next he turned his head toward me. He grabbed my hand and shook it firmly, looking me in the eye. Once again, he shifted his gaze to Montel, looking knowingly into her eyes as he held her hand and paused. Finally he released her hand and proceeded out of the church.

We were amazed that he had stopped and acknowledged only us and primarily Montel. Did he somehow know this was the daughter of the distraught father he had talked to several months ago? Had he been praying for this girl the whole time and now knew his prayers were answered, seeing she was at home with her family where she belonged?

This incident and others made us feel as if we belonged in church. Over the next several years, we kept attending more and more frequently. It was as if we were being gently drawn into the church not by force, but by attraction. We started noticing that we always felt better after attending mass.

By the time Montel was around three years old and Sean was two, I had completed graduate school and successfully moved my career to information technology.

By then we had pretty well settled into a weekly routine schedule. Delia and I worked all week, did a variety of errands and chores on Saturday and then attended church on Sunday. Probably seven out of every eight Sundays it was mass at eight o'clock followed by breakfast at a restaurant that we had dedicated to be our Sunday-after-mass-breakfast-restaurant, the Corner House.

The Corner House was an old house that had been converted to a restaurant. All of the windows had comical paintings of an artist's renderings of fish, steak, and chicken. The hand-painted windows also touted their specials. When you walked into the place, the atmosphere was friendly and casual. We were generally greeted by Beverly, a heavy-set, short Italian woman with a warm smile, and her friendly demeanor was pure and sincere. The Corner House had a very unique décor. The walls were decorated with stuffed fish and birds. The entire interior of the structure that had apparently once been a house was filled with booths along the outer walls and interior frame. It was a little bit run down; however, it was neglected in a good way. The fastidious nature of Beverly and the staff, wiping and mopping all of the time, made us confident that it was a clean restaurant. But a missing floor tile here or there, a burned out light on part of their neon sign, made it feel run-down enough to be totally comfortable and relaxing.

Yes, our Sunday routine was complete: church followed by breakfast at the Corner House. And over the years, we had even been designated our own waitress. Not really, but we couldn't tell Lavern that. Lavern was an old woman who had a wrinkled face and deep voice from years of smoking. She was as tough as nails on the outside, but we knew better. Lavern always asked how Montel was doing and told us she admired us for taking such good care of her. Lavern told stories about how she had encouraged a friend of hers to keep a son who had Down syndrome rather than give him up for adoption. She was one of the pioneers that pushed the school board to allow her friend's son the right to attend regular school. She understood a lot of the issues that we faced with Montel and was always encouraging and supportive. If Lavern had a weakness, it was that she was a bit possessive. When we first started going to the Corner House, we did not concern ourselves with whether or not Lavern was working and, at times, we would let someone else wait on us. Lavern would see us and would come over to our table and lecture us for not sitting in her section. Well, we were quick learners, so, after a few times, we knew the drill. Go to the Corner House, find out what station Lavern was working, and, for Heaven's sake, don't sit anywhere other than in her section!

And as the years passed, Montel grew and developed into a beautiful little girl that, while small for her age, had flawless, light olive skin, beautiful auburn hair, dark penetrating eyes, and slightly high cheekbones that gave her just a hint of her Asian ancestry. She had long legs and was always every bit the little lady. She loved dressing up in different clothes and liked to be pampered. She also enjoyed swimming and being taken outdoors.

Montel would develop normally for a period of time and then stop. The path of her development was full of brief spurts of rapid development followed by what seemed like endless plateaus. For example, she was able to stand holding onto something when she was less than two years old. I recall excited conversations and letters to friends predicting that she would be walking soon. But at four and a half years old she was still only able to stand with support, virtually no change.

One particular morning after church, I pulled the car into the parking lot of the Corner House and carried Montel out of the car and into the restaurant. Once inside I spotted Lavern, and she pointed to a table at the end of the row of booths to my left. Montel started squirming and wanting to be free. I put her down and let her stand holding onto a railing near the entrance.

I walked to the end of the aisle between the booths fully expecting Delia to come in after me carrying Montel to our table. But as I got to the end of the row, I saw an excited and shocked expression on Lavern's face as she looked down the aisle that I had just walked. I turned around and everything in my entire world shut down except for Montel. I had complete tunnel vision locked onto her. She had a look of utter determination and resolve as she awkwardly moved one foot forward, paused to catch her balance, and then repeated the process with the other foot. I could not believe it . . . Montel was walking! They were ill-at-ease, wobbly and awkward looking steps, but Montel was walking! She continued to struggle forward, one tiny step at a time, until she reached me and latched onto my leg. She looked up at me and her face lit up with a smile. My narrow focus on only her was suddenly shattered by the sound of clapping. I looked up, and, led by Lavern, the entire restaurant, seeing what had just happened, had burst into applause. It was a dizzying and surrealistic feeling to be standing there with Montel as the entire restaurant, staff and patrons, looked at us smiling and applauding. I looked around at all of the faces full of love and affection and realized that in seeing Montel walk for the first time, we had all just witnessed a miracle, and we knew it.

Another memorable time of Montel's life came several months later when she was about five years old. We decided to go out for pizza one evening. Nothing seemed unusual about the evening as we got into our car to go out. It was a typical pleasant but overcast late afternoon in the Bay Area as we headed south to a pizza parlor that we had been to several times in the past. So as I got out of the car and headed into the restaurant, I had no reason to suspect that events inside would give me a new insight into Montel's abilities.

When we arrived, we split up with Delia and the kids

staking out a booth while I walked up to the counter to order. I ordered our usual pepperoni pizza and drinks, and then joined them at a booth near the video games. The booth's location was undoubtedly selected by Sean. While waiting for the pizza, I began to occasionally hear outbursts from a large group of people seated at one of the large tables two or three booths down from where we were seated. I really didn't pay much attention to them at first. But as the outbursts became more vocal and more frequent, my curiosity got the better of me, and I turned around to get a look at this noisy party.

One glance and I knew this group was not your local neighborhood softball team celebrating after a game. I saw a group of about six to eight rough looking bikers. The women had stringy unkempt hair, and the men looked tough and bitter. All of their faces were hard and weathered. One large man was seated in the middle of all of them, and he appeared to be the ringleader. He was a mountain of a man wearing a leather vest that showed off his huge, heavily tattooed arms. One of his biceps had a tattoo of a heart with a banner over it that read, "Born to Kill." The other bicep had a tattoo of a skull with knives for crossbones. There were many other smaller tattoos on his arms and neck. His eyes were intense with anger and hate. To the left of the leader was a very tough looking Hispanic man who had two teardrop tattoos below one of his eyes. I remembered hearing somewhere that each teardrop tattoo below an eye represents each time the person has killed someone. Looking into the emptiness of this man's eyes I immediately believed it.

I turned back around quickly and felt as if we should leave to avoid trouble. But I ignored these feelings, rationalizing that while they may not be people that we would want to meet in a dark alley, if we maintained a low profile and kept to ourselves, there should not be any trouble.

As time progressed, however, they became louder and more rowdy. And I began to realize just what kind of element we were dealing with here. Apparently I was not alone in my growing concern about this group because steadily people left the restaurant until no one was left but them and my family. I started overhearing pieces of their conversations with references to release dates, drugs, and the names of some cities that just happen to house some of the toughest prisons in California. Then at one point the leader got up to get another pitcher of beer. As he returned to his table with the pitcher he looked at me as he crossed in front of our booth and barked, "What are you looking at?!"

"Nothing," I said, as I looked away from him. Thankfully he proceeded to his table. But I got the feeling he would have preferred that I give him a reason to show me what those tattooed 18" weapons for arms of his could do. This definitely seemed like a man who was very angry at the world, and it was probably only a matter of time before he would do something to prove it.

Once he returned to the table, the group continued to be loud and intimidating. The owner was standing behind the counter now watching them and obviously not sure exactly what he should do. The leader looked right at the owner and proceeded to light up a cigarette defiantly right in the restaurant. Smoking in a restaurant is illegal in California, and by the threatening way that the leader looked at the owner as he lit up he no doubt knew the law. His expression seemed to say, "Go ahead . . . try to do something, and I'll return later tonight and firebomb this place!" The owner turned away pretending not to see anything. Frankly I would have done the same thing . . . I have seen plenty of punk kids trying to act tough, but I was convinced this group was the real thing. These were some bad hombres.

They continued making loud outbursts of mean-spirited laughter. I forced myself to ignore them. On the one hand, I was reassuring myself that nothing would happen to us as long as we did not do anything to provoke them. On the other hand, I felt as if there was bound to be trouble with a group like this because I had the distinct feeling they were looking for it.

What happened next was really unconscionable on my part. Delia got up and left the booth for some reason. I may have been distracted by watching Sean wander over to the video games. Or maybe it somehow didn't fully register that Delia had gone, and I thought she was still watching the kids. Or maybe I just became lost in thought and forgot to keep an eye on Montel. Whatever the reason, I looked over at the seat on the other side of the booth and realized Montel was not in her seat! My heart raced with panic. I looked over at the video games hoping she was with her brother, but only Sean stood at one of the games. I started scanning the restaurant to see where she might have gone. As if the terror of having a non-verbal daughter wandering around lost was not scary enough, when I finally spotted her, it was worse. She was standing at the table right between Mr. Leader and Teardrops! I was horrified.

"Great," I thought. "This is all I need." I could just imagine how this could be twisted around to become some kind of huge invasion of their privacy, thereby justifying my being beaten to a pulp. But no matter how much I wanted to avoid that table, I knew that I must approach them. This was my daughter after all.

I stepped up to the table prepared to give an apology that would make pleas given under flashing lights to avoid a speeding ticket pale in comparison. But once I got to the table, I realized something was very different. The table was quiet and everyone at the table was fixated on Montel. The leader looked up at me from Montel, and the expression on his face had completely changed to one that was relaxed and soft - downright kind. I surveyed the table and realized all of them looked completely different than they had before as they gazed upon Montel. The women looked upon Montel with kindness and joy written all over their faces. And the men replaced their harsh and intimidating demeanors with relaxed expressions of awe and compassion. Montel was smiling at them and seemed to be soaking up all of the attention.

The awkward silence was broken by the Leader as he looked up at me.

"She ain't quite right is she bro'?" he asked.

"No," I said as nonchalantly as possible. "She has a disability."

"Well, she sure is a pretty little thing," he said, as he smiled kindly, looking back down at Montel.

I stood there in shock at how civil this group now seemed. But I flashed back to my assessment of how awful and dangerous this table was, and so after a moment that seemed like forever, I started trying to leave these people as discretely as possible.

"Well," I finally said, "I guess we better go."

At that, Teardrops took my hand and looked deep into my eyes with the blackest eyes I have ever seen. The same eyes that earlier were completely empty and void of emotion now conveyed a deep sense of love. "God bless your soul, sir," he said with deep sincerity. "You're doing a wonderful job with that little girl." He continued to hold eye contact and my hand for a moment longer before repeating, "May God bless your soul."

I was stunned! I thanked him and walked away not quite sure what to think about the change in these people. I was still thinking we should probably get the heck out of there before there was trouble for reasons I couldn't possibly explain. Then I thought perhaps I had misjudged the table in the first place. The table burst into a loud explosion of laughter. I turned around and scanned the table. They once again fit into my original assessment and conclusion that these people were a gang of ex-convicts and thugs.

I gathered the family and started heading towards the car. I was feeling a sense of urgency, but again, for no apparent reason. As we got to the car, I was still trying to register the dramatic transformation I had just witnessed in those people back inside. Delia commented on how scary they were.

Driving home I continued to try to make sense of what had

happened. At this point, all I knew was that even though I had witnessed it with my own eyes, it was hard to imagine people changing that dramatically. Had I really misjudged those people that badly? I reminded myself of their rough and vulgar mannerisms and language, not to mention the multiple references to prison, drugs, and violence. Then I started to see the irony of the situation. I was limited in my ability to see these people for who they really were because, unlike Montel with her so-called disability, I could only judge them based upon what was showing on the outside. I looked back at Montel in the rearview mirror. She looked up and gave me a knowing smile.

From that day forward, I understood that Montel has a very unique ability to see people on some sort of deeper, spiritual level than most people see. It is as if she has a little spirituality barometer that she can use on people. I have seen her immediately befriend some rather unruly looking characters while rejecting very respectable looking ones. And over time I have observed that all of her assessments ring true.

CHAPTER 7
FULL CIRCLE

When Montel was around six years old, we were at a city park that was hosting a local carnival. There were colorful booths with homemade carnival-style games for the children to play and big barrel barbeques cooking hamburgers, hotdogs, and ribs.

I was standing next to a large jumping trampoline contraption for the children that was a blown up balloon rendition of a dragon. Montel was bouncing on it. I stood among a crowd of people, and I was looking for where my son, Sean, had wandered off to, when out of the muffle of voices from the crowd I heard something that briefly caught my attention. But I was too distracted looking for Sean to really discern exactly what it was. A moment later I heard it again, but again I could not make it out. It was as if a single word or words would jump out at me from the background noise of all of the people talking and children playing, but I couldn't tell exactly what it was that kept getting my attention. Finally I saw Sean over by a basketball throwing arcade game with Delia when I heard it again.

This time I turned and saw what kept bothering me. A cute little blonde-haired girl about seven years old was playing on the trampoline along with my daughter and several other children. She was holding her hands up and pushing them out to warn the other children to keep away.

"Stay away from that *handicapped* kid," she said, cautioning the other children as she signaled with her open hands, monitoring a six-foot perimeter that she had formed around my daughter.

I think I was as surprised as the little girl by how harshly and quickly I responded to her. I did not have time to temper my tone of voice or reaction to be appropriate for a child. Instead I brusquely blurted out my automatic response.

"Excuse me!" I said. "Her name is Montel."

Hearing those words come out of my mouth reminded me of the argument I had with Delia years before when Montel was in the hospital, and it made me realize that I had completely transformed. I no longer viewed Montel in terms of her disability, but instead I saw her as a complete human being. There was no one incident, or even several incidents, that changed my attitude about people with severe disabilities like Montel. Although the priest pausing in church, the dramatic way Montel walked for the first time, and the incident with the bikers at the pizza parlor were all memorable, none of them could have made me start to see her as a whole person. No, it was not anything dramatic or sensational that brought me around to a new way of thinking.

What changed my attitude about Montel was the way, year after year, I would see rough looking kids pause and drop their tough-guy routines for a moment at the very sight of Montel. As if a part of them deep down inside acknowledged, "There but for the grace of God go I." It was my brother-in-law, the stoic former marine, whose face filled with compassion at the first sight of Montel, as he mumbled to himself, "She's your miracle baby." It was the countless people who held doors open, or patiently waited as we slowly made our way up steps, or simply nodded reassuringly and lovingly at the mere sight of Montel.

But mostly what changed my attitude about Montel was just being around her. The way when she smiles her whole face smiles; she gets dimples on both sides of her mouth and her eyes become little slits. And the way she walks up to me and unexpectedly gives me a hug and pats me on the back. What changed me is how when we ask Montel, "Who's pretty?" She smiles and points to herself. And the way when she laughs it is a release of pure joy; her body shakes and her head bobs with complete, uninhibited delight. I was changed by the way she has so much compassion for other people; she cries when her brother gets a scolding. It's her quirky mannerisms, like sometimes walking up to family members and kissing them on both cheeks and then on the lips for no apparent reason. And her cute little personality, like when you catch her doing something she knows is wrong, she stops dead in her tracks and smiles sheepishly. And I was changed by her love which is absolutely pure and unwavering: Even when she is bed-ridden with a high fever and sickness, she will roll her eyes to look up at me as she gives me a little smile.

So it was not any one event, but the cumulative effect of years and years of small events stemming from being around Montel. I now saw her as a complete and perfect human being. I realized that even though everything in the medical journal article that I read years before was technically correct, it was not accurate. It only described the physical, tangible aspects of Montel which happen to be her poor qualities. Who among us would look good under such scrutiny? When describing Montel one has to also consider her intangible qualities: her wonderful loving spirit, her optimistic personality, and her innocent loving nature.

CHAPTER 8
THE BEGINNING

B ack in the director's office with the coffee all gone, and several breaks later, Julie said, "In other words, at some point, and you're not exactly sure when, you finally saw your daughter as a complete person?"

"That's right," the director said.

"But your wife saw her that way all along?" she asked.

"Yes she did," he said. "Basically when it was time to take Montel home from the hospital she outsmarted me, thank God, and prevented me from making the biggest mistake of my life. I will always be grateful to her for that. She gave me the space I needed and allowed me to grow into a person who could accept my daughter. It made me gain a deeper level of respect and love for my wife than I had for her before Montel was born. Don't get me wrong; I always knew that she was an incredible person. I just hadn't realized how incredible until Montel was born."

"But," she said, "I'm still confused on how you got from accepting Montel as a person to starting a home, especially one as innovative as this one."

"I would say mostly it was how much love and acceptance we got from people regarding Montel that inspired me. After years of witnessing people reacting to Montel with warm smiles, tender looks, and a loving understanding and helpfulness, I began to realize that most people nowadays appreciate the special qualities of these unique people with developmental disabilities. It got me thinking: If social attitudes can go from putting the mentally retarded into institutions, to so much tolerance and understanding in just one generation, why couldn't we take it to the next level and have these people far more integrated into our society during our generation? So when we began the home I insisted we have at least one guest room. Many people told me, and sometimes with great passion, that it was a complete waste of real estate. And in the beginning I must confess it did seem a little extravagant, since most of the time it sat empty. Then slowly, family members of our residents began to warm up to the idea, and they'd stay with us. Soon more and more family, friends, and even acquaintances of our residents would stay. Eventually we needed more rooms for our guests, until we ended up with as many guest rooms as residential suites. Now the guest rooms are always full, and they usually need to be reserved several months in advance. And as you can probably tell by your tour, it completely changes the dynamic of our place from a typical care home to more of a vacation atmosphere."

"It sure does," Julie agreed. "I especially noticed that in the swimming pool area. Everyone seemed genuinely relaxed and having so much fun that I almost dived in myself!"

They chuckled for a moment, and then at the same time they both seemed to realize they had better get back to the business at hand, which was seeing if Audrey could get into the home.

Julie spoke first. "What else do I need to do as far as my daughter?"

"Well," the director said, "You will need to complete the application package. But, even before you do that I should tell you our philosophy of taking care of our residents," he said. "Let me explain a typical day that your daughter would have here at the ranch . . . not today, a weekend, or a holiday either, but a typical day. We take a holistic approach to caring for our residents. Real simple to remember: P.I.E.S. P is for physical. We make our residents work out at least two hours a day. Everything from simple exercises in the pool for some of the more challenged individuals . . . to going to our weight room and pumping iron for the more hardy souls. Don't worry Julie;

we won't kill your daughter. But we do find out what she is capable of doing, and we expect that she exercise to the best of her ability every day. If you want your daughter to sit and be a vegetable all day this is the wrong place."

He paused to study her reaction. Once he was satisfied that he hadn't already frightened her off, the director continued: "I is for intellectual. Again we have a large range of abilities here. So to some of the residents this is time when a staff member reads to them. Others read themselves, write, or work on communication skills. But the point is that all of them need to be working toward personal achievement goals every day."

"E is for emotional," he said. "I'm sure Brandy told you we highly encourage visits from family and friends. You have my word that we will do our best with your daughter . . . but no one can love her like family. In addition to the visits, we involve the community around here as much as possible. We arrange for visits from the local schools, and encourage seniors in our area to visit and spend time with our residents. I absolutely refuse to accept the idea that these people need to be isolated from the general public. I find that idea highly offensive and believe with all of my heart that the more our residents are woven into the fabric of our society the better our society will become. Does the prospect of Audrey interacting regularly with so-called *normal* people concern you?"

"Absolutely not," Julie replied. "I thought I was going to have to strangle a school principal one time because she was trying to block me from getting Audrey into a mainstream classroom."

They both laughed and had a good feeling for one another. A special relationship had formed between the two as they recognized the common bond they shared as parents of special needs children.

"Finally, S is for spiritual," the director continued. "We take all of our residents to a church of your or the guardian's choosing as often as practical . . . usually at least three times a month. We believe these are special people that are in God's hands. Most children grow up, have free will, and make their own choices. But people like your daughter are so special because they remain in God's hands forever."

Julie's face dropped, and she asked, "What if I told you that I'm an atheist?"

"No problem," the director assured her. "Attendance to church on Sunday is purely optional. The bottom line is this Julie: This is not a care home where we take care of the basic sustenance of your daughter and call it caring. Here you are becoming a part of our family. A family with similar ideals, desires, and goals for our special needs family members. Of course we will have differences, but our core values have to be the same. And these are our core values: We believe that people with special needs deserve to be treated with dignity, respect, and love. We believe that these people need to have the protection, structure, and sustainability of an institution such as this one. But that in no way implies that they should not be as integrated and socialized with the general community as much as possible. Our residents are valued, contributing members to society. People in the little town you drove through on the way here know our residents by name. In working with the leaders of that community we find ways for our people to contribute. It was difficult for the community to think of our residents as having anything to give in the beginning; but over the years the town's people have discovered that they are the bigger beneficiaries of this relationship." He paused and then said, "I think what I'm mostly trying to say is that we believe above all else that special needs people are just people. We think that society tends to overreact and behave as if it is a really big deal to have them around. Here is one little spot on earth where it is not a big deal. People don't come here to be with people that have disabilities any more than they go to other places to avoid people with disabilities. Here it is simply not a big deal either way."

He paused as he thought of a way to illustrate what he meant, then began again. "If a forty-year-old mentally retarded man wants to play on the swing-set in a typical city park, people will probably *allow* it, simply because the laws say they must, or they are too embarrassed to say anything. But watch how everyone looks away ashamed, and how many conversations end in an awkward silence as people begin to notice. But that same man gets on a swing here and we not only allow it, we provide oversize swings and *encourage* it! No one gets embarrassed or takes his or her children away. Most often some child will see him and run over to the swings to join him! The point is, here at this ranch, on this little forty acres of the world, we refuse to overreact to someone's disability. It simply is a non-issue. And we are committed to promoting that position. While we never envision a day when people will jump for joy when they discover that their newborn baby has some type of problem that will leave him or her with a permanent disability, we do envision a day when the rest of the world will be like our little forty acres is now, and it will not be the end of the world. The disappointed parents will recognize that while this may not be the baby of their dreams, they will also know that he or she will grow up to be a protected, loved, and contributing member of society."

"Rest assured Mr. Evans," Julie said earnestly, "we have the same core values."

They talked some more and before the director said good bye, he gave her the large envelope containing the application package, instructing her to return it as soon as possible. She was relieved to hear that due to the fairly rigorous prescreening process that she had already been through over the phone prior to coming up here, he didn't foresee any reason why Audrey would not be accepted into the home.

Julie headed out of the French doors of the common room to the courtyard. She saw that Audrey was still sitting with the group in the courtyard holding hands with Rachel and smiling. It had been a long time since Audrey had smiled.

Julie retrieved Audrey and as they made their way back out to the parking lot, she saw the sign over the parking lot attendant and made a pushing motion with her hands, indicating that she did not want her *"preconceived ideas and biases,"* returned. She felt like they were entering into a new and exciting phase of Audrey's life.

They got into the car and made their way back out of the private driveway of the ranch. Driving away, the road didn't seem to be nearly so bad. The pot holes weren't as big, the pavement wasn't as rough, and it was not as narrow as she remembered it being when they arrived. In fact, she now noticed how beautiful the wild flowers along the road were, and what lovely rolling hills and oak trees formed the contour of this landscape.

As she meandered down the country road back home, she flashed back over Audrey's life: how her husband had left her, the years of hard work fighting school boards and demanding services, and the cursed last few years when the little yellow bus quit pulling up in front of her house and Audrey wasted away for hours at a time in front of the television. She considered the lovely place where Audrey now seemed to fit right in, and it seemed that there was at last a silver lining to the years of challenge caused by Audrey in her life. She approached the main road and had to pull over to wipe the tears of gratitude from her eyes.

Blessings in disguise are difficult to recognize

God sends his 'little angels'
In many forms and guises.
They come as lovely miracles
That God alone devises.
For He does nothing without purpose
Everything a perfect plan
To fulfill in bounteous measure
All he ever promised man.
For every 'little angel'
With a body bent and broken
Or a little mind retarded
Or little words unspoken
Is just God's way of trying
To reach and touch the hand
Of all who do not know him
And cannot understand
That often through an angel
Whose wings will never fly
The Lord is pointing out the way
To his eternal sky
Where there will be no handicaps
Of body, soul or mind
And where all limitations
Will be dropped and left behind.
So accept these 'little angels'
As gifts from God above
And thank him for this lesson
In Faith and Hope and Love.

Helen Steiner Rice

Printed in the United States
53380LVS00002B/34-84

9 781598 002294